# THE
# LITTLE BOOK
## OF
# HORRORS

# THE
# LITTLE BOOK
## — OF —
# HORRORS

SCARY TRUTHS THAT WILL
MAKE YOU FEEL LUCKY TO BE ALIVE

STEVEN MARR

CASTLE POINT BOOKS
NEW YORK

THE LITTLE BOOK OF HORRORS.
Copyright © 2024 by St. Martin's Press.
All rights reserved. Printed in the United States of America.
For information, address St. Martin's Publishing Group,
120 Broadway, New York, NY 10271.

www.castlepointbooks.com

The Castle Point Books trademark is owned by
Castle Point Publishing, LLC.
Castle Point books are published and distributed by
St. Martin's Publishing Group.

ISBN 978-1-250-36764-8 (hardcover)
ISBN 978-1-250-34752-7 (ebook)

Our books may be purchased in bulk for promotional,
educational, or business use. Please contact your local bookseller
or the Macmillan Corporate and Premium Sales Department at
1-800-221-7945, extension 5442, or by email at
MacmillanSpecialMarkets@macmillan.com.

First Edition: 2024

10 9 8 7 6 5 4 3 2 1

# CONTENTS

# INTRODUCTION

**Life is scary.** That's what our mothers, movies, school assemblies, and commercials for drugs to treat diseases we've never heard of have all taught us. Plus, evolution has trained our minds to imagine all kinds of threats as a way of preparing us for every possible impediment to our survival. There's a reason nobody turns on the lights in a spooky movie: it could illuminate whatever ghastly ghoul or bug-eyed murderer is lurking in the gloom. While that would be terrifying, isn't it ultimately less frightening to see the danger than to worry about it?

That's where *The Little Book of Horrors* comes in. Collected here are **hundreds of the most truly strange, awful, and ridiculous ways to die,** from eating too much licorice or being clobbered by flying turtles to ticking off soldiers under your command or being hit by a meteorite. You heard me—*meteorite*. Yes, many of these are chilling to consider. But some are funny and fascinating. And none are more horrific than living in the dark.

Just being conscious of the fact that any of us could drop dead of an undetected embolism at any moment (you're welcome) doesn't keep it from happening. Spend all day looking up for falling pianos, and you'll eventually walk into traffic. But knowing what's out there and not letting it control you can help make the world that much less alarming. And understanding some of the many, *many* ways our lives can come to an end may even help you appreciate what you have just a bit more. So, think of this book as the heroine flicking on a light switch in the haunted house and saying, **"Hmm. Could have been worse."**

"Do not take
life too seriously.
You will never get
out of it alive."

—ELBERT HUBBARD

## Chapter 1

# EVERYDAY
# HORRORS

# Drinking yourself to death doesn't always involve alcohol.

Water is life, yes? You can only survive three days without it. But moderation is key. Take, for example, the California woman who drank six liters of water in three hours as part of a radio station contest to win a Nintendo ("Hold Your Wee for a Wii") in 2007. She died from water intoxication. That's when you guzzle huge amounts of water so fast that **the liquid overloads your kidneys, sometimes leading to brain swelling** and, in a few cases, death. On the bright side, you're far less likely to embarrass yourself on the dance floor with this kind of intoxication.

# A gallon of carrots a day can put you underground.

An obituary for Basil Brown of Croydon, England, described him as a health-food enthusiast. But that may have been an understatement. His "enthusiasm" was so pronounced that **the coroner described the cause of death for the forty-eight-year-old scientist as "carrot-juice addiction."** Brown was drinking about a gallon daily. The vitamin-A overdose acted just like alcohol poisoning. Like many addicts, Brown ultimately died of cirrhosis of the liver. Whether the bright yellow tint of his skin was due to jaundice or juice is anyone's guess.

> *"Life is short and I don't want to*
> *miss out on eating dessert."*
> —DAVID NIHILL

## Switch to red licorice.

In January 2019, a seemingly healthy fifty-four-year-old Massachusetts construction worker was in a McDonald's when he lost consciousness. He was **pronounced dead at the hospital from multiple-organ failure and hypokalemia** (a dangerously low level of potassium). A mystified doctor, finding that the man's diet included lots of candy, wondered if licorice might be to blame. Hypokalemia can be triggered by "excessive consumption" of glycyrrhizic acid, the active ingredient in black licorice, specifically. The man had been eating one or two packs of the soft candy daily, which was enough to do him in.

## Labels save lives.

Twenty-five-year-old Ukrainian student Vladimir Likhonos was studying at home when his life ended in catastrophe. He was chewing gum, which he liked dipping in citric acid to boost its sour taste. As habits go, this one was unusual, even by the standards of chemistry students. But it wasn't harmful—until one night in 2009, that is. After hearing an explosion, **his mother found Likhonos on the floor, his jaw blown off.** It turns out, Likhonos had accidentally dipped his gum not in citric acid, but in an unlabeled explosive powder used for his studies.

# No one expects to be taken out by a cork.

Do you duck when a friend gets a little too enthusiastic with a bottle of champagne? You should. Dozens of people have suffered serious eye injuries from high-speed champagne corks unleashed without consideration for innocent bystanders. Impaired vision and even blindness aren't uncommon, and **particularly nasty complications have occurred when the cork smashes through a person's eyeglasses.** Sadly, there's no available information on the quality of the weaponized champagne. (You'd hate to lose an eye for subpar bubbles.)

# Turn off the stove and open a window.

Gas stoves may be the darling of every home-improvement show, but they've been making headlines in recent years for their hazardous health effects. Parts of the developing world where families cook on stoves using smoky fuels like wood or kerosene have it even worse. The problem is poor ventilation, which traps deadly fumes inside. A National Library of Science study describes **these silent killers as many times more dangerous for children than even being around parents who smoke cigarettes.** It makes up the bulk of over 3 million premature deaths attributed to household air pollution each year.

# Even pastry comes with risks.

Most visitors to Las Vegas don't realize the MGM Grand casino is not the original. The first MGM was a luxury property built further north on the Strip in 1973. It was also the site of the worst fire in Nevada history on November 21, 1980. **A blaze sparked by a malfunctioning pastry case in a casino restaurant ripped through the MGM's high-rise tower,** aided by the lack of a structure-wide sprinkler system. Despite heroic efforts by volunteers and a squadron of military helicopters trying to save those trapped on the high floors, eighty-seven people died, most from smoke inhalation. Because some things only change after tragedy, these days every floor of every Vegas casino and hotel has sprinklers.

## SURVIVAL TIP

House fires account for 92 percent of civilian fire deaths. Put the odds back in your favor by staying low, closing doors behind you, and placing a wet towel under the door. (And go put new batteries in your smoke detectors *now*.)

# Waking up on time is important, just not *that* important.

A newspaper account from 1886 told the story of Long Island's Samuel Wardell, who had a hard time getting up in the morning. (Relatable.) So Wardell rigged up a Rube Goldberg–type device with an alarm clock connected to a weight that was designed to fall onto his headboard loud enough to wake him up. After a Christmas party at his house, he failed to notice somebody had moved his bed. When Wardell's alarm went off the next morning, **the weight fell not on his headboard, but on his head.** While sleeping through your alarm is a problem, it is harder to get up for work when you are dead.

# Beauty should not be pain.

Not so long ago, fashion could be fatal. In the nineteenth century, many women wore tight-laced whalebone corsets, which created a visually flattering hourglass figure but also crushed internal organs and cut off blood and oxygen. **Newspapers carried stories about corseted women dropping dead.** In one famous 1894 case, a married couple was performing a play in London when the wife collapsed offstage and died after the second act. A doctor later determined that her tight corset had exacerbated her heart condition. The husband and the rest of the cast were "understandably very distressed," but they went ahead and performed the rest of the show.

# Where's the safety on this thing?

We can make machines to do a lot of things, but that doesn't mean we should. Take the Oerlikon GDF-005, for example. It's an automated anti-aircraft gun that uses radar and laser finders to identify and target enemy aircraft and missiles before blowing them out of the sky with its 35mm cannons. That's what the brochure said, at least. But in 2007, one of the Oerlikons bought by the South African military **malfunctioned during a training exercise.** Instead of hitting dummy targets, it tragically killed nine soldiers. (It's as though nobody has ever watched the first *RoboCop*.)

# Gargoyles are terrifying for many reasons.

The Second Presbyterian Church on Chicago's South Michigan Avenue has some of the city's most beautiful architecture. Built in 1874, it's a gorgeous Gothic Revival structure with a remodeled Arts and Crafts interior, complete with pre-Raphaelite murals. As was discovered one afternoon in 2014, though, the stone gargoyles adorning the bell tower could have used some extra attention. That day, **part of one came loose and plummeted down,** fatally striking thirty-four-year-old Sarah Bean and unlocking a new fear for city-dwelling pedestrians.

# Look out below!

Gargoyles are not the only things that have been known to fly off places of worship at unexpected times. On a summer morning in 1989, a fourteen-year-old girl named Martine Blot was standing by Paris's Notre Dame cathedral with her tourist group. Unbeknownst to her, a man had chosen that moment to end his life by leaping from the top of the cathedral. **He landed on the girl with crushing force, killing them both instantly.** Oddly, this had happened before: an American tourist in 1964 and a Canadian tourist in 1983 were both killed by people jumping to their death from Notre Dame. Perhaps, at some point, a warning sign would be appropriate? "Watch for falling bodies!"

## Peter Pan syndrome is dangerous.

It was a perfectly unremarkable day at Yankee Stadium in 1999. The Bronx Bombers were playing the Toronto Blue Jays. While this was going on, an adult male who did not have the excuse of being inebriated was sitting on the handrail of a down escalator. Then something unexpected and yet entirely predictable happened: he fell. **And because he fell 90 feet onto a hard surface, he died.** Fortunately, nobody else was injured by the falling man, who knowingly risked his life for a childish whim.

## This is not so much tempting fate as goading it.

In 1989, convicted murderer Michael Anderson Godwin had reason to celebrate. He had originally been sentenced to death by electric chair. But a retrial, while still finding him guilty, changed his punishment to life in a South Carolina prison. **The electric chair was still waiting for him,** though, in a manner of speaking. One day, sitting naked on his cell's metal toilet and trying to fix his broken headphones, as one does, he stuck one of the wires in his mouth (again, totally normal) and promptly died from electrocution.

## Give the coffin a good shake.

In October 1571, a funeral procession was carrying the body of Matthew Wall—a young farmer who had been found "dead"— to be buried at the church in Braughing, England. Fortunately for their cargo, one of the pallbearers slipped and dropped the coffin. **The assembled party was surprised to hear a knocking from *inside the coffin.*** Wall turned out to be just fine, thank you very much, though in another hour, he might not have been. He lived another twenty-four years, though one wonders what he thought every time he went to sleep.

# Being almost killed can end as badly as being killed.

Unfortunately, nearly being buried alive hasn't been relegated to the days before modern medicine. It's happened as recently as 2014, when Paul Mutora "died" of an attempted suicide by poisoning. His family came to view his body at the morgue in Naivasha, Kenya, and then went home to plan the funeral. That's when the supposedly dead Mutora started calling for help. **The mortuary assistants quite wisely ran away screaming.** It turned out Mutora had been given a drug at the hospital that slowed his heart rate so much that he only appeared dead. Perhaps some of the hospital staff slept through the "How to Tell Whether Somebody Is Dead" seminar.

# Have you noticed your walls glowing?

Things went bad fast for a family who moved into a new apartment in Ukraine's Donetsk region in 1981. The eighteen-year-old daughter died that year, followed soon after by her sixteen-year-old brother, and then their mother—all from leukemia. Then neighbors fell ill. After another family moved in, *their* teenaged son died. To dispel rumors of a curse, investigators studied the apartment in 1989 and **discovered a tiny capsule packed with the radioactive isotope Cesium-137 embedded in the wall**. The capsule had been accidentally bundled with building materials from a nearby quarry, where it had been used as part of a measuring device. Why builders seemingly just shrugged their shoulders after losing a potentially lethal tool is a question for another day.

# You never want to have a syndrome named after you.

Medical examiners studying a person who died from sudden accidental strangulation may refer to it as "Isadora Duncan syndrome." This is because of the terrible way the glamorous, world-famous dancer lost her life in 1927. Duncan was being driven in a new convertible along the Riviera in Nice, France— not a care in the world—when her trademark long silk scarf caught in the car's back wheel. **The scarf snapped tight around Duncan's neck, yanking her out of the vehicle.** She died instantly from strangulation. Ominously, the previous day, she said she was scared "some quick accident might happen."

# They're all bad options.

The history of capital punishment is also the history of attempting to find more supposedly humane methods of carrying out a death sentence. During the nineteenth century, hanging seemed the most common way of dispatching convicts. Firing squads were also popular; while more labor-intensive than hanging, both methods shared a low equipment threshold (rope, bullets) and seemed relatively quick. In the twentieth century, **electrocution, poison gas, and lethal injection** were all promoted as more merciful ways of killing. But it's now known that each new method has the potential to cause excruciating agony—meaning your best bet is to just never get convicted of murder (or, you know, never *commit it*). Especially in Texas.

# You'll shoot your eye out.

Long before Ralphie begged for a Red Ryder BB gun in the movie *A Christmas Story*, kids were being told they would maim themselves with that toy. But there's good reason for the warning: around 30,000 people go to the emergency room in the United States every year after being shot with non-gunpowder rounds (ball bearings or pellets). **High-velocity versions of BB guns kill about four Americans each year.** And at close range, BB rounds can cause as much damage as low-velocity bullets. Almost all these injuries are sustained by boys aged ten to fourteen years. So if you see an adolescent boy waving a BB gun around, duck!

# Humans lack wings for a reason.

BASE jumpers are a special breed. The acronym stands for the places they like leaping from: buildings, antennas, spans (bridges), and earth. Many of them think nothing of hopping off a mountain as if they were a large-scale flying squirrel, with **just a wingsuit to keep them from splatting on the ground**. Things do not always turn out their way, though: in the summer of 2016 alone, over thirty BASE jumpers met their demise in unfortunate yet highly predictable and gravity-related ways. It's gotten so bad in recent years that some jumpers want separate fatality statistics for BASE jumpers who use wingsuits, lest those who use parachutes be lumped into the sport's bad press with their more impulsive colleagues.

# Maybe don't do unnecessarily dangerous things.

Many extreme sports could be better described as "feats of painful endurance." Free diving is among them. That's when people with ridiculous lung capacity compete over how deep they can **dive underwater without any breathing apparatus.** Unsurprisingly, this does not always go well. In 2001, free diver Jay Moriarity—also a renowned surfer who had barely survived wiping out on the feared fifty-foot Mavericks wave off Santa Cruz—died when free diving alone in the Maldives. His fatal accident is used today as an example of why the buddy system remains necessary at any age.

# Keep the party indoors.

It was after midnight at a party on Chicago's North Side in 2003 when the building's overcrowded third-floor balcony collapsed, crushing two balconies beneath it. Dozens were injured, and thirteen people died. According to an Associated Press analysis, **roughly 6,500 people were injured and 29 killed by balcony and porch collapses** in the United States between 2003 and 2015. The number of casualties related to this kind of accident is high enough, in fact, that there is an entire subset of personal injury lawyers and law firms that advertise themselves as specialists in deck, balcony, and porch collapses. FYI: The view is just fine from *inside* the building.

# Always listen to the engineers.

The Verrückt (that's literally German for "insane") waterslide at Schlitterbahn Waterpark near Kansas City was unlike anything else in the world. Almost 170 feet high, it was the tallest slide of its kind, sending people flying down its chute at up to 70 miles per hour. Engineers warned that its design almost **guaranteed that rafts would go flying off the chute,** but operators went ahead. In 2016, a raft carrying a ten-year-old boy went airborne, sending him to his death. Schlitterbahn co-owner Jeff Henry had once said he built his rides based on "trial and error." Following this tragic and unnecessary "error," the Verrückt was dismantled.

# This high is not worth the pain.

Drug-addiction specialists are always coming across new substances they need to watch out for. Some are dangerous, others strange, a few are both. In the mid-2000s, doctors in eastern Russia began seeing gross **splotches of dark, scaly, and almost reptilian skin** on drug addicts' corpses. This was an aftereffect of "krokodil," a drug cocktail that mixed codeine with a batch of toxic nastiness that included red phosphorus scraped off matchboxes. The drug's popularity may have waned due to side effects ranging from crocodile-like skin lesions to zombie-like necrotic leg ulcers. And no amount of lotion was going to mitigate that.

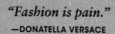
*"Fashion is pain."*
—DONATELLA VERSACE

## What wouldn't you do for fashion?

Oscar Wilde was one of Victorian England's most well-known wits, but not many people remember his ill-fated sisters. His father, Sir William Wilde, had two daughters out of wedlock: Emily and Mary. On Halloween 1871, Mary was dancing with a man at a ball when a candle ignited her dress as she swirled past it. Emily ran to her sister, only to have her dress light up as well. **The sisters died weeks later from the burns.** The culprit was identified as their fatally fashionable flowing crinoline skirts. This material was so well known as a fire hazard that, in 1858, *The Tablet* magazine darkly joked that ladies wearing it "should be accompanied by a footman with a pail of water."

## Is there a wrong hand?

It has been often said that 2,500 left-handed people die every year from using equipment created for the right-handed. While this exact figure is in dispute, the issue it highlights is not. In 1991, The *New England Journal of Medicine* mentioned a study showing **right-handers live on average about nine years longer than the left-handed.** The researchers suggested one reason for left-handed people's increased mortality could be that more of them had accident-related injuries, most likely because of the world's right-handed design bias.

# The comedian who cried heart attack.

A mainstay of the standup circuit, raunchy comic Redd Foxx achieved stardom on *Sanford and Son* in the 1970s. On that show, one of his signature gags was pretending to have a heart attack. He would stagger around, shouting, "It's the big one!" That might be why his **colleagues assumed he was joking when he collapsed** during rehearsals for his new show, *The Royal Family*, in 1991. The sixty-eight-year-old died from his very real heart attack at the hospital shortly thereafter, proving that it's unwise to tempt fate, even when acting.

## SURVIVAL TIP

There are many signs of a heart attack besides crushing chest pain—especially for women. Knowing the subtler warnings can save your life (or someone else's). Shortness of breath, fatigue, sweating, nausea, dizziness, heartburn, jaw pain, and back pain can all be precursors to "the big one."

# Walking along cliffs
# is hard enough.

Thanks to the impossible-to-match hype leading up to its 2001 release, the Segway two-wheel self-balancing scooter was destined to be something of a joke. The company fell on hard times before being bought by British millionaire Jimi Heselden in 2009. About a year later, Heselden was riding a Segway on a path near his West Yorkshire home when he suddenly reversed course to make room for a man walking his dog. This small act of kindness, which would have been nothing had Heselden been on foot, cost him his life. **He tragically plunged over 30 feet to his death.**

# There must be easier ways
# to get rich.

Three men in the quiet German town of Schoppingen had a plan for the heist of a lifetime. The idea was to put a bomb on a condom vending machine, blow open the machine's door from a safe distance, collect the money inside, and live happily ever after. On Christmas Day 2015, the men put their plan into action. But the bomb exploded early, **sending a piece of shrapnel into the head of one of the robbers,** who later died. In their rush to escape and take their unlucky friend to the hospital, where they would tell an unbelievable cover story, the thieves left a pile of money and condoms for authorities to find.

# Read the fine print on those hospital forms.

In Belgium, euthanasia is legal for patients with an "incurable disorder" who want to end their life and avoid further suffering. But some doctors may have taken the law further than intended. A 2015 study reported it was possible that thousands of people had been subjected to "involuntary euthanasia," which is another way of saying **the doctors killed them without first receiving consent.** A few years earlier, over a hundred Belgian nurses said they had taken part in euthanasia that patients may not have agreed to. In their defense, not everyone has the ability to communicate in the end, and the nurses believed they were following the patients' wishes.

# Don't pick a fight with a vending machine.

In 1988, the Journal of the American Medical Association featured an article about an unusual but very real problem. In the appropriately titled "Soda Pop Vending Machine Injuries," Dr. Michael Q. Cosio explained discovering an odd phenomenon while working at the Walter Reed Army Medical Center. Cosio studied fifteen male patients aged fifteen to twenty-four, all of whom were **severely injured by vending machines they were trying to tip over.** Three died, including one "found pinned to a wall with the soda machine resting on his neck." In fact, several dozen people have lost their lives while stealing from vending machines, which feels like too high a price to pay for a free soda.

# Just to be safe, take a shower.

People tend to take showers to get clean and take baths to relax. However, some might be relaxing a bit too much. The problem with bathtubs and hot tubs is so pronounced, in fact, that roughly one person dies every day in the United States from drowning in one of them. At least a few of these deaths are intentional. But the issue is worse in the western states, where **people are more likely to combine their bathing and hot-tubbing with drinking and drugs.** There are, unfortunately, no statistics on whether bubble baths are more dangerous than those sans suds.

## When experts start shouting, there's usually a reason.

FBI agent John P. O'Neill had spent years hunting Al Qaeda before most people had heard of them. A legendary counterterrorism expert, O'Neill spent the 1990s investigating Muslim extremists and fighting against a lack of support in the agency. After working on the 2000 USS *Cole* suicide bombing and amidst tension within the bureau, he retired on August 22, 2001. On August 23, 2001, O'Neill started a new job: chief of security for the World Trade Center. He began warning people about an impending Al Qaeda attack. O'Neill **was last seen walking toward the South Tower on September 11, 2001,** after the North Tower's collapse. His remains were found in the wreckage on September 21.

# Watch where you step.
# Forever.

While trying to stop the North Vietnamese from using Laos as a highway to the South between 1964 and 1973, the United States dumped over 2 million tons of explosives on the neutral country. That's more than all the bombs dropped during World War II combined. A lot of those bombs never went off and are just waiting for some curious child to try and play with them. Since the end of the war, **at least 20,000 Laotians have been wounded or killed by the unexploded ordnance.** But some industrious, risk-tolerant Laotians still use them for scrap metal, art supplies, and building materials.

# Caffeine can kill you.

Caffeine-related deaths tend to be accidental, like the case of the Welsh personal trainer who miscalculated the amount of caffeine powder he put into a workout mixture. He died soon after, **having ingested the equivalent of nearly 200 cups of coffee at once.** The coroner later noted the trainer had "got his maths wrong." Since the advent of energy drinks, it's gotten even easier to underestimate your caffeine intake. In 2023, two people died after drinking Panera Bread's "Charged Lemonade," which exacerbated their underlying health conditions with its more than 200 mg of caffeine.

# Take a nap instead.

"Ventricular arrhythmia" was one of the more common causes cited in a 2021 cardiovascular medicine journal for a "fatal outcome." The cause? Energy drinks. Because of the rapidly expanding market for these caffeine- and sugar-loaded drinks, some health professionals have begun cautioning patients on the increasing health risks. In 2011 alone, **more than 1,500 teens went to the emergency room for energy drink–related problems.** And according to the Center for Science in the Public Interest, at least thirty-four people died from them over a ten-year period. If you really need the pick-me-up, just get an espresso.

# Is that half-price juicer worth your life?

On the hallowed holiday of Black Friday, people still digesting their Thanksgiving dinner line up at malls and big-box stores in the wee hours as they wait to fight over heavily discounted goods in a pre-Christmas shopping frenzy. Over the years, at least seventeen people have died and more than a hundred have been injured in this strangest of rituals. **Some have been trampled, and others have been shot, stabbed, or beaten in altercations.** Stores still try to stoke the Black Friday fires every year, but, thankfully, you can find most shoppers safe at home, yelling at their computers instead of their fellow consumers these days.

# All I want for Christmas is a fake, nonflammable tree.

Before electricity was invented, people lit up their Christmas trees the only way they could: with candles. While pretty, combining open flames and dry pine had predictable outcomes. In 1925, a Christmas-tree candle sparked a conflagration in an Oklahoma schoolhouse packed with holiday revelers, killing thirty-six people. These blazes were so common that insurance companies stopped covering Christmas-tree candle fires. But don't let your guard down just because you use electric lights. **Holiday pines continue to kill.** In one estimate from the early 2010s, six Americans die annually in Christmas-tree fires. (Go water that tree.)

## SURVIVAL TIP

Dry trees aren't the only cause of Christmas-tree fires—25 percent are the result of electrical problems or, more commonly, decorations getting too close to heat sources. To keep your holiday from going up in flames, check light cords for damage, make sure they're not getting hot, and unplug them overnight and before leaving home. And no matter how ugly they are, do not tuck extension cords and power strips under the tree skirt.

# That 72-inch screen isn't worth it.

Advances in entertainment technology have turned household televisions from cathode-ray tubes in big wooden boxes sitting on the floor to sleek flat-screens mounted on walls. This has been great for both home decor and binge watching. It's also probably been good for keeping people alive. During the 1990s and 2000s, hundreds of children died each year from furniture falling on them, often heavy old cathode-ray tube TVs that tipped over. **As recently as 2011, twenty people died from having a TV fall on them.** By the year 2020, the number was down to three. Just remember to secure that flat-screen to the wall—watching *Ted Lasso* isn't worth your life.

# Go touch grass.

Studies on the loosely defined issue of Internet Gaming Disorder have identified something called "sudden gamer death." Most causes have been attributed to a combination of sedentary behavior, dehydration, sleep deprivation, and high stress from the gaming itself. South Korea saw an acute case in 2002, when twenty-four-year-old Kim Kyung-Jae collapsed at a twenty-four-hour internet café. He then went to the bathroom, where he was later found dead. Police said **the tenacious gamer had been playing for eighty-six hours straight,** without eating or sleeping. They did not say how far away he was from the high score.

> *"You may hate gravity, but gravity doesn't care."*
> —CLAYTON M. CHRISTENSEN

## Remember, boomerangs are designed to come back.

Boomerangs are fun, but they do come with warnings, such as "can cause harmful, even serious, injuries" (per the United States Boomerang Association). As far as we know, boomerang injuries are not fatal. Unless your name is Kaakutja. That is the name given to the prehistoric skeleton dug up in Australia's Toorale National Park in 2014. With **a boomerang-shaped gash across his skull,** he is the first (and only) recorded human killed by such a weapon. The mouth of Kaakutja's skull is wide open, possibly to register shock at the very strange way he was about to die.

## Watch out for flying lawnmowers.

In 1979, New York Jets fans had little to cheer about, given the team's unremarkable stats. The Jets eked out a win in a home game they played that December 9 against the New England Patriots, but the events of that game were nothing to celebrate. The halftime show that day featured a display of remote-controlled model planes. One of the planes, **a heavy, mostly metal, two-foot-long model shaped like a lawnmower,** went off course and slammed into the stands, hitting two fans. One survived, but the other died from his head injury several days later.

# Flammable things
# are everywhere.

William Kogut was a murderer slated for the noose at San Quentin prison in California. Instead of enjoying his final days, he got tired of waiting for his execution and decided to take care of things himself. His planning was extensive, if demented. On the night of October 19, 1930, Kogut packed a mash of water and torn-up playing cards into the hollow leg of his cot. Why cards? At the time, the red ink in playing cards was made with a volatile compound. He then **set his head against the improvised explosive** and ignited it with a small heater. Prison personnel found him bloodied and dead in his cell in the early morning hours of October 20. At least the hangman got the day off.

# A book on the nightstand
# might be safer.

In December 1992, Ken Charles Barger of Newton, North Carolina, was sleeping when the phone next to his bed started to ring. He grabbed for the phone to see who it was. But he never found out. That is because he had left his Smith & Wesson .38 Special by the phone. **Accidentally grabbing the revolver instead of the phone,** he put it to his ear. The gun went off, creating both a tragic accident and a gun-safety advertisement at the same time.

# Never trust someone who says, "Trust me."

After World War II, the Central Pacific's Marshall Islands came under the authority of the United States, which decided to use it for nuclear testing. Once locals were removed from Bikini Atoll and Enewetak Atoll, dozens of bombs were set off. After testing ended in 1958, the U.S. military sent thousands of personnel to clean up the sites. With many empty promises of safety, yet almost no protection, the men **dumped radioactive material under a massive concrete dome.** Years later, those same men began getting cancer at alarmingly high rates, earning the Marshalls a designation as one of the most, if not the most, dangerous island chains in the Pacific.

# Take the toothpick out first.

Toothpicks are handy little things, mostly for holding big, messy sandwiches together. Researchers have even uncovered evidence they were used by Neanderthals (though probably not for club sandwiches). But an astonishing number of people are injured every year by **poking themselves with or swallowing a toothpick.** A number in the thousands. And an average of three people each year die from those injuries. In 1941, the great American writer Sherwood Anderson—who once said "The thing, of course, is to make yourself alive. Most people remain all of their lives in a stupor."—died of peritonitis caused by accidentally swallowing a toothpick at a party.

# That's a long way down.

As with other death-defying activities, people involved with skydiving like to say how safe it is. Still, when the fatalities occur, they are terrifying to imagine. Every year since 2020, roughly ten to twenty people die while skydiving. The most commonplace **causes of these fatalities involve the diver smacking into something**—like a tree or a building or just the ground—at a high rate of speed. Every now and again, skydivers will land in the water and drown. But, in those cases, at least their chutes were working, and they got to enjoy the scenery on the way down.

## It can't hurt to stock up on first-aid supplies.

Wars have been raging across the earth almost since man first stood upright and narcissistically declared ownership of the land under his feet. Despite advances in technology and emotional intelligence, things are getting worse, not better. The year 1994 was particularly terrible for humanity, with almost 800,000 people dying in various conflicts. According to the groups who track wars and related miseries, things leveled off somewhat after that. But after 2020, **the number of state-based conflict deaths around the world began spiking starkly.** Continuing a bad trend that does not appear to be abating, 2022 turned out to be this century's worst year so far as it pertains to people's chances of dying in war. So maybe the preppers have a small point.

# This seems like the opposite of the point.

First devised by inventor Jack Cover in the 1970s, the Taser is a handheld device used by police as a nonlethal weapon. **It fires darts that deliver a paralyzing 50,000-watt electric charge to a person's nervous system.** Tasers were initially seen as a humane alternative to subduing people with clubs or firearms, but they have been connected to least a thousand deaths since they were widely adopted in the early 2000s. Police fatally shoot roughly that many people every year with firearms, so the Taser is an improvement. But the original idea for the Taser was zero fatalities. (Maybe lower the voltage?)

# And you thought *waking up* involuntarily was annoying.

People with narcolepsy, a condition that scrambles the brain's ability to regulate sleep, often have a hard time staying awake during the day. They can unwillingly fall asleep while standing up or even in the middle of an activity, like driving. This often-lifelong condition has no known cure. And it can lead to terrifying problems for people like Allison Burchell, whose **narcoleptic cataplexy—a variant that can cause paralysis—led her to be pronounced dead three times.** Even though she could hear what was happening, her body would not respond. (A big tattoo that reads, "I have narcolepsy, don't bury me too quickly" might be advisable.)

# Unfortunately, doctors are just humans.

Those who feel just fine going to the doctor or the hospital for simple procedures might want to be more nervous. **Doctors and nurses make mistakes.** A lot of them, it turns out. A 2023 Johns Hopkins study calculated an overall error rate of 11.1 percent. It also estimated that wrong diagnoses kill 371,000 Americans every year and permanently disable another 424,000. (Maybe there's a reason lawyers chase ambulances.)

# So are paramedics.

Many people in medical crisis relax once the ambulance arrives, but ambulances kill people, too. In 2021 alone, thirty-nine people were sent to an early grave because of crashes involving ambulances. (Fire trucks, which seem more dangerous due to their size and speed, only killed twenty-four that year.) A story from 2023 is especially concerning: After a deadly crash that March, it was later alleged the teenaged ambulance driver was going 20 mph over the speed limit when he **dropped his phone and veered into oncoming traffic.** The paramedic in the back and another driver both died as a result.

# Holidays are hard on the heart.

The holiday season in the West comes packaged with a host of tension-causing factors. Given that, plus the many gatherings, people tend to overindulge on food, treats, and drinks. It should come as no surprise, then, that **the worst day of the year for cardiac deaths in America is Christmas Day.** Doctors have termed the surge of patients with irregular heart rhythms "holiday heart syndrome" and blame it mostly on a combination of copious amounts of alcohol and dehydrating salty foods. If you don't want to spend next Christmas in the emergency room (or the morgue), take it easy on the eggnog and cheese platter.

## SURVIVAL TIP

Not only do doctors make mistakes, but racial and gender biases are huge problems in healthcare. Advocating for your health is crucial, and a second opinion never hurts. If a doctor refuses to order a test or medication you think you need, ask them to document it in your chart. You'd be surprised how many reconsider.

# Mass hysteria is a real problem.

Many concert disasters are caused by patrons rushing to get out (often, away from fire). But one of the most disturbing nights in music involved them trying to get in to watch The Who's December 3, 1979, show at Cincinnati's Riverfront Coliseum. People waiting for hours in the cold began agitating when it sounded like the band had started. Then two doors opened, and the crowd surged forward. In the mayhem, caused in part by general admission ticketholders rushing for good seats, **eleven people were killed by trampling or suffocation.** The Who played their show, unaware of the tragedy, because their manager was worried that cancellation would cause a riot. Cincinnati's mayor told the Associated Press that concertgoers had "lost all sense of rationality."

# Are you dying to get some sleep?

Nearly everyone has had insomnia at some point, and it's usually nothing to fear. Usually. But then there's sporadic fatal insomnia. It is an extremely rare disease—less than forty cases have been identified in the United States—but it's also extremely awful. A subtype of sporadic Creutzfeldt-Jakob disease, it's caused by a spontaneous mutation that attacks the thalamus and **progresses quickly through loss of coordination, extreme insomnia, coma, and death.** A similarly rare syndrome called fatal familial insomnia is just as bad and is an inherited condition, which at least gives you someone to blame.

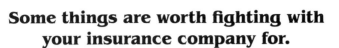

# Some things are worth fighting with your insurance company for.

One of the worst things about cancer is just how many versions of it there are. About 2 million people are diagnosed with cancer annually in the United States. **More than 600,000 Americans die from it each year.** Thankfully, some types of cancer are more beatable than others. The ones with the best survival rates are thyroid and prostate, with 98 percent and 97 percent, respectively. One of the more deadly cancers is colorectal cancer, and it's on the rise, thanks largely to humanity's increasingly poor habits. Should you eat better and exercise? Sure. But you should also get screened either way.

## Pass the broccoli.

Smoking is really, really unhealthy. Everybody knows that by this point, right? (Hence lung cancer topping the list of deadly diseases.) Yet enough people are still carrying on with smoking that it kills about 8 million of them a year. However, cigarettes are still not as dangerous as a bad diet. **Between obesity and related diseases, roughly 5 million people die every year** from eating too much of the stuff they know they shouldn't eat and not enough of the stuff they know they should. That should put things into perspective for people who look at smokers with disgust on their own way through the drive-thru.

# Evolving technology means evolving safety warnings.

People have been fascinated by X-ray machines since their introduction in 1896. There were practical uses for this technology, like identifying broken bones. But there were also less practical uses, like the shoe-fitting fluoroscope, **a type of machine that used X-rays to determine a customer's exact shoe size.** Though mostly useless, customers loved it so much that about 10,000 shoe stores carried them by the 1950s. As understanding about the dangers of radiation exposure spread, the machines were quietly retired from stores. Nobody has any idea if or how many people developed cancer from using one.

# Games involving projectiles are generally pretty risky.

Paintball has the advantage of seeming a lot like combat—running around with realistic weapons trying to "kill" opponents—but with no risk. Yet there is always some risk. In 2004, the Contois family had taken their ten-year-old son to a paintball park for his birthday. During the game, a fourteen-year-old player accidentally dislodged a valve on his gun, and **the gun's $CO_2$ canister shot out at a high velocity.** It hit Mrs. Contois in the head off-field, killing her almost instantly. Sadly, hers wasn't even the first death by a $CO_2$ canister-turned-projectile.

# Toys were like
# this once.

Americans once thought it was just fine to give their children lawn darts. These were metal-spiked mini-javelins with arrow-like fins that you flung into the air so they would land inside a plastic hoop with **their sharp metal points stuck in the ground.** One day in 1987, some kids in Riverside, California, were playing with lawn darts when one accidentally struck a seven-year-old neighbor in the head, killing her. The weapon masquerading as a toy was banned the following year. However, some families either never got that news or chose to ignore it and kept on letting their kids throw around sharp metal objects at will.

## Teenagers should be
## bubble-wrapped.

The fact that body armor isn't actually bulletproof does not seem as widely known as it should be. On April 3, 2022, fifteen-year-old Christopher Leroy Broad of Belleview, Florida, found this out the hard way. He came to the hospital with a gunshot wound and died that night. Not long after, police determined what happened: Broad and his friend, seventeen-year-old Joshua Vining, had **taken turns putting on a body-armor vest so the other could shoot them** with a handgun while another friend recorded everything on video. One shocked neighbor chalked it up to teenage-boy behavior.

# Not "the talk" you were expecting.

Suicide among adolescents most commonly happens by firearm. Another frequent method of suicide is suffocation, generally done by hanging. However, a closer look indicates that not all these hanging deaths are intentional. One study found that, over a ten-year period, **roughly one-third of all adolescent deaths from hanging were attempts to achieve autoerotic asphyxia.** This is incredibly dangerous, especially when performed alone, which is why anywhere from 250 to 1,200 deaths a year are attributed to autoerotic asphyxia in the United States. So add that to the list of awkward-yet-imperative sex-related things to talk to your kids about.

# Don't play with deadly things.

Most fatal shootings involve one person intentionally aiming at another person or group of people. Sometimes, though, the person who gets shot has nobody to blame but themselves. In 2019, for example, there were 486 unintentional gun deaths in America, which was about 1 percent of all gun deaths. One study indicated that roughly **a quarter of those deaths resulted from playing with the gun,** and 6 percent just from dropping it. Drinking was frequently involved. So next time you feel like playing *Charlie's Angels* in front of the mirror, you may want to wait on the beer.

# Always check credentials.

The Super Bowl halftime show tends to be its own kind of awful, but it has one saving grace: nobody dies. Usually. The 1997 Super Bowl show at the New Orleans Superdome included a few Blues Brothers, James Brown, and a number of stunt performers. During final rehearsals, **bungee jumper Laura Patterson hit her head on the Superdome floor** after too much jumping cord was let out. She died soon after. It turned out that the person in charge of her jumping cord was an untrained volunteer—two words you never want to hear attached to death-defying activities.

# Watch for flying pucks!

Throughout hockey history, there has been a rule for fans (announced before each game): keep an eye out for pucks shooting off the ice. This changed in March 2002 at a game in Columbus, Ohio. **A slap shot deflected by a defenseman rocketed into the stands,** fracturing the skull of thirteen-year-old Brittanie Cecil. She died in the hospital two days later. Soon after, the National Hockey League (NHL) began installing safety netting in every arena and raising the height of the protective glass around the rinks so no one would have to test their reflexes against flying pucks again. People who obviously prefer a greater risk of random death complained.

"When I die,
I want to die like
my grandfather,
who died peacefully
in his sleep. Not
screaming like all
the passengers
in his car."

—WILL ROGERS

## Chapter 2

# TRAVEL IS A NIGHTMARE

# Traveling by horse and carriage suddenly sounds more appealing.

The first automobiles appeared on British roads in 1895. It took time for people to understand what these rarely spotted machines were. In August 1896, a car being driven around the Crystal Palace exhibition hall ran into and killed Bridget Driscoll. **She became the first known auto-related fatality in the United Kingdom.** By the time statistics were first compiled three decades later, nearly 5,000 British people were being killed in auto accidents every year. How many people wisely started taking the Tube when those numbers came out is unknown.

# Seat belts save lives . . . most of the time.

The seat belt is one of the most amazing lifesaving inventions in human history, cutting the number of fatal injuries from car crashes roughly in half since its introduction. But it comes with a cost. When a fast-moving car hits an object, the human passenger is hurled forward, putting pressure on each part of the body touching that three-point adult harness. That causes "seat belt syndrome," which can be **anything from bruised skin to fractured ribs and major damage to internal organs.** Only one person has died from it, though—a driver in Tehran with critical damage to his neck, likely caused by an improperly worn seat belt. Of course, the man was also driving roughly 110 mph at the time of the crash.

# Freedom means never having to click it.

Just a few short decades ago, Americans weren't legally required to wear seat belts. Some people (and one state—New Hampshire) never relented to the change. One of those Never Seat-Belters was Derek Kieper, a University of Nebraska-Lincoln senior. In a 2004 op-ed for the *Daily Nebraskan*, Kieper declared, "And if I want to be the jerk that flirts with death and rides around with my seat belt off, I should be able to do that, too." The following January, **a beltless Kieper died after being thrown out of a car during a rollover;** two seat-belted passengers survived. (Sometimes the endings write themselves.)

# The Pinto is why safety ratings exist.

In the 1970s, Ford Motor Company was very happy with sales of their budget-priced subcompact car, the Pinto. But Ford had a secret: the Pinto's affordability was in part due to the company skimping on safety. That became headline news in 1977, when *Mother Jones* cited a whistleblower claiming **at least seventy people a year were dying from Pintos exploding,** primarily from rear-end collisions that hit the car's unprotected fuel tank. (Further investigation found twenty-seven Pinto-related deaths, which is still too many.) It was an easy $11 fix, but Ford chose a slightly higher profit margin over customers' lives until they were forced to announce a recall. Ford stopped making the cars soon after, in 1980.

# Do you trust technology with your life?

In theory, with Tesla's Autopilot, you can plug in your destination, sit back, and let the car do the rest. In theory. In reality, the software doesn't work exactly as planned, **leading to approximately forty deaths** connected to Autopilot-driven cars. One problem: The software's guidelines tell drivers to keep their hands on the wheel and their eyes on the road. While clearly safer, this does undercut the benefits of using the software in the first place. Which is why some drivers unwisely ignore the guidelines . . . to their own detriment.

# What you don't drive can hurt you.

The first "self-driving" car known to have killed a person actually had a human driver at the time. On March 18, 2018, the ride-share company Uber was test-piloting the car in Tempe, Arizona. Though it was in "autonomous" mode, the car was being monitored by a so-called "safety driver." **Nevertheless, the car ran over and killed a bicyclist**—forty-nine-year-old Elaine Herzberg. The utility of having a safety driver on board seemed to be diminished by the fact that, when the crash happened, she was watching the talent show *The Voice* on her phone (although her attorneys claim she was only listening).

> *"The best car safety device is a rear-view mirror with a cop in it."*
> **—DUDLEY MOORE**

## Yield to emergency vehicles.

One of the most thrilling parts of many movies is when the cops chase the bad guys. But the reality is that many people end up injured or dead in those high-speed car chases—and not just the bad guys. In fact, **525 people were killed in 2021 from vehicle accidents caused by police chases,** 21 percent of them innocent bystanders. Most of these chases involved non-violent—and sometimes very minor—crimes, making the body count even more egregious. So if you hear sirens, move away fast.

## Geography matters.

Statistics are compiled for every subject you can imagine. That includes death. The Centers for Disease Control (CDC) studied data about causes of death between 2001 and 2010, identifying the most disproportionate outliers in each state. This is how we know that, even though most people died from heart disease or cancer, there was an unusually large number of deaths from **the flu in Maine, accidental gunshots in Alabama and Tennessee, and syphilis in Louisiana.** All of which is pretty useful information when you're thinking about traveling out of state.

# Take GPS directions with a big grain of rock salt.

Sergey Ustinov and Vladislav Istomin were driving across the frozen bleakness of Siberia along Kolyma Highway in 2020 when Google Maps told them to take a shortcut. This mostly unpaved road, which cut through **some of the world's most inhospitable territory,** was known as the "Road of Bones" due to the remains it contained of the thousands of workers who died building it under orders from Josef Stalin. The road had been abandoned and treacherous since the 1970s. Unfortunately for the unprepared teens, their car broke down. Ustinov froze to death in the -50°C cold. Istomin, thankfully, was rescued and fought his way back from acute hypothermia.

## SURVIVAL TIP

Never underestimate extreme weather. The car might be nice and toasty, but if it's freezing outside, dress like it. Or at the very least, keep blankets, boots, and coats in your trunk alongside water, food, and some kitty litter (for traction of course; what were *you* thinking?). And if you're going to be traveling in a remote area, bring flares, a full tank of gas, and a battery-powered phone charger.

# Don't use cutlery while driving, obviously.

Keeping two hands on the wheel is basic stuff. At the same time, it's not advice everyone follows. One such rebel was a twenty-eight-year-old man driving a Lexus in San Diego early one morning in February 2022. He collided with a parked vehicle hard enough to create a five-parked-car chain reaction and set off his own airbags. **The driver later expired at the hospital.** The scene baffled investigators at first, given the stab wound in his neck, the knife and pooled blood in the car, and no apparent assailant. Investigators pieced together the evidence and came up with a theory: The driver crashed while using the knife to mix a protein drink.

# Keep your head on a swivel (and on your body).

In collisions, people in the smaller and/or lower vehicle are more likely to end up dead. That rule of thumb is especially true in what safety experts call "underride collisions." This is when a car collides with a large truck either from the back or the side and slides under it. **The car's windshield and top are often smashed or even entirely sheared off**—sometimes along with the passengers. Despite regulations requiring underride guards (which, it's worth noting, often fail when hit at high speed), over 400 people still died this way in 2021 alone.

# They call them "donor-cycles" for a reason.

There's no denying that motorcycles are awesome. The chrome, the big handlebars, the blasting sound of the engines, the way they look when roaring in a big pack of black leather and attitude down the highway—it's all thrilling. But that coolness comes with a hefty price (and not just the sticker shock you get at the dealer). Motorcycle riders are about **thirty times more likely to die** in an accident than if they had been in a boring old car. That minivan may not look exciting in your driveway, but it is way less likely to leave you smeared along the highway.

## Seriously, wear a helmet.

Though it has never quite taken off in the United States like it has in other places (China or Amsterdam, for example), bicycling has enjoyed a boost of popularity recently. But though bicycle trips make up just one percent of trips in the United States, they comprise two percent of fatalities in auto-related accidents. Of the roughly 1,000 bicyclists who die every year, the victims are overwhelmingly men; **male bicyclists have fatality rates roughly seven times that of their female counterparts**. No one knows why, but the prevailing theory among cyclists is that men take more risks with their safety. (But anyone who has seen a YouTube video could have told you that.)

> "*The one thing that unites all human beings . . . is that, deep down inside, we all believe that we are above-average drivers.*"
> —DAVE BARRY

## Next time, take city streets.

Anyone who's ever driven along I-95 knows what it's like to take their life in their hands. That's especially true for those who have to drive the one-mile stretch in Fort Lauderdale between I-595 and State Road 84. A 2022 study discovered that section had the unfortunate distinction of being **the deadliest road in America,** clocking twenty-four fatalities between 2000 and 2019. A safety advocate sagely told a local paper, "There are deficiencies." In fact, all ten of the deadliest stretches of highway in the study were in Florida and Texas. (Something to keep in mind when planning your next road trip.)

## Amazingly, the explosives aren't the biggest risk.

Based on a 2021 study, you should stay home on Independence Day in America. It's not that the colorful explosives could rain down on you, although it's happened. It's that the Fourth of July is one of the most dangerous holidays to be on the road—second only to New Year's Eve. There are so many drunk drivers on that supercharged summer holiday that **your chances of being killed by one of them are about 20 percent higher** than on an average day. If you want to go driving on a holiday, stick with the safest one, which is, surprisingly, Christmas.

## You have died of dysentery.

Before American Airlines, the way to get across North America was to hitch up Bessie to the family wagon and follow a trail west. A quarter to a half million people crossed the continent on routes like the heavily traveled Oregon Trail of pixelated video-game fame. It was a hard journey. **Around 10 percent of pioneers died on the roughly 2,000-mile journey from disease alone.** Of course, there were gunshot deaths, drownings at river crossings, and animal attacks, as well. But due to nineteenth-century sanitary conditions surrounding water, cholera—not dysentery—was the main killer. (Sorry, '90s kids.)

## Talking like a movie supervillain is a big red flag.

Germanwings Flight 9525 from Barcelona, Spain, to Dusseldorf, Germany, on March 24, 2015, should have been routine. Little did passengers know that, before the flight, copilot Andreas Lubitz had been **researching cockpit door security systems and suicide methods.** Once the pilot left the cockpit, Lubitz locked him out. Lubitz then flew the plane into a mountain in the French Alps, killing all 150 occupants. It was discovered Lubitz had a history of depression and had told an ex-girlfriend, "One day I will do something . . . then everyone will know my name and remember it," just like a rational person who should be responsible for people's lives would say.

# Even pilots make mistakes.

When a Yeti Airlines plane crashed in Nepal in January 2023, killing seventy-two people, it was a great tragedy. But its cause may have been painfully banal. As the plane was coming in for a landing, and it was time to adjust the wing flaps, **one of the pilots moved the wrong lever.** The engines stalled and the plane smashed into the ground and burst into flames. Unfortunately, the odds were never in the travelers' favor. Nepal is regarded as one of the world's most dangerous countries for flying, even when pilots keep their levers straight.

# Death by explosive decompression on a plane sucks.

Explosive decompression on an airplane will not kill you. Usually. Of course, it's never good when something punctures an airplane. The pressurized air inside the cabin can then get sucked out as though a massive vacuum were pulling it—and every loose object—outside, leading to confusion, panic, and things blowing around inside the cabin. Every now and again, though, people are hurled out of the plane thousands of feet above the ground. And on one unfortunate Southwest Airlines flight in 2018, **shrapnel from an exploding engine crashed through a window, causing gale-force winds to pull a woman partially out of the plane.** Even though her seatbelt kept her lower half inside, she still died from the blunt-force trauma. Just in case you needed something else to worry about while you're shooting through the air in a tin can at 30,000 feet!

# Better to annoy your seatmate than die of politeness.

Deep vein thrombosis (DVT) is a fancy term for blood clots that form in "deep veins" (the ones farther under your skin). Usually, they just dissolve on their own. But in worst-case scenarios, you get a pulmonary embolism. This is when a clot travels and causes a blockage, which can be fatal. **As many as 300 people a year die from embolisms,** and those flying long distances are at greater risk. You can improve your chances of avoiding a clot by shifting your legs often, plus walking around, during a flight (or anytime you're sitting for long periods). That might be annoying, but it's better than dying or having your leg amputated after a cross-Atlantic flight like British passenger Val Clark in 1995.

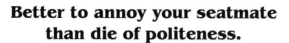

## SURVIVAL TIP

Your odds of surviving an airplane crash get lower the farther your seat is from an exit row. If you can't sit by an exit, count the rows to the nearest one so you can reach it in the dark if you need to. The same principle goes for fire exits in a theater; the fewer people you have to climb over, the better.

# Train travel has its own downsides.

Early in the evening of January 27, 1947, two young boys decided to have some fun with materials the Pennsylvania Railroad had left by one of its tracks in Walton, Indiana. They piled wire fencing, pieces of wood, and piping on the rails. Minutes later, a westbound, eight-car passenger train came along at about 60 mph in the hazy weather. **The train derailed, killing three passengers and the crew's fireman, and injuring close to forty others.** This happened just ten days after a train wreck in Bakersfield left seven dead and about three weeks before another train wreck in Altoona, Pennsylvania, killed seventeen. Still, trains are as much as fifty times safer than cars, which is food for thought.

# The minibar isn't just pricey.

Stories about people dying on vacation usually involve cruise ships or wild animals (don't worry, we'll get to those). But in 2019, an unusual story came out of the Dominican Republic, where tourists kept dying at different resorts. Hearing some guests had felt ill after drinking from their minibar, a *New York Post* reporter investigated. **They noticed a strange smell, like methanol**—an ingredient used in antifreeze—which suggested the resorts were serving counterfeit booze. The resulting poisoning was probably an unintentional by-product. The possibility of drinking antifreeze might be just one more reason to avoid the minibar.

# Quarantine is no one's idea of a vacation.

People boarding the cruise ship *Grand Princess* in San Francisco on February 21, 2020, couldn't have known that dozens of people on the ship's just-concluded trip had come down with COVID, and some would soon die. Days into their own cruise, the *Grand Princess* was ordered to wait off the California coast so test kits could be delivered via helicopter. On March 9, the ship finally docked in Oakland, where several thousand passengers continued to be quarantined on land for two weeks. **More than 120 infections and at least 6 deaths were connected to the *Grand Princess* outbreak.** Proving memories are short, unlimited buffets tempting, and risk calculations often faulty, several passengers from the fated cruise reported they couldn't wait to get back on board just a year later.

# Take it easy on the poolside mojitos.

Even considering COVID-related illness, your odds of dying on a cruise are very low—1 in 6.25 million. But a 2020 *International Journal of Travel Medicine and Global Health* article helpfully broke down *what* people die from on cruise ships. About a quarter of the 623 deaths identified between 2000 and 2019 came from falling overboard or onto a lower deck, while **about 18 percent came from "suicide, murder, and a terror attack."** While some might find it reassuring that only one terror attack on a cruise ship occurred during that time, others may prefer to just go to Six Flags instead.

# Oxygen is a nonnegotiable.

Ads enticing tourists to beachy locations inevitably show happy people scuba diving in crystal-clear waters. Understandably, they do not show the people who die while enjoying that idyllic-seeming activity. When the Royal College of Pathologists of Australasia dug into how people expired while scuba diving, they discovered **causes that ranged from stingray wounds to head injuries from boat propellers.** But they determined that most deaths were due to a "critical error" in judgment, particularly running out of air. So if you're the distracted type, stick to the beach.

# This is one wave you don't want to wipe out on.

For surfers who spend their days looking for towering waves on which to delicately balance themselves, the pastime can turn deadly in a heartbeat. (And not just because of shark attacks.) The north shore of Hawaii's Oahu is prized for its surf reef break, the Banzai Pipeline. The "Pipe" is as dangerous as it is famous, **having killed at least seven surfers in the past few decades**—more than any other wave in the world—and injured many more. Whether this makes it more gnarly or less is a question best left to surfing lexicographers.

# At least they'll have a nice picture for their obituary.

New technology has probably created as many problems as it has fixed. One growing issue is the dangerous selfie. People are increasingly putting themselves in risky situations just to get the right shot, sometimes with deadly consequences. A 2021 study published in the *Journal of Travel Medicine* estimated that **379 people had died because of taking selfies** between 2008 and 2021. Though the study found that women take more travel selfies overall, it's not entirely surprising that most of the dead were men nineteen years or younger. The most common cause of death was falling from a high place mid-pic, but posting selfies while driving deserves an honorable mention.

## They died doing what they loved.

The Chausey Islands off the coast of Normandy, France, is the kind of place that often gets called an "off-the-beaten-path gem." It is generally not called a "romantic hook-up spot." But that is apparently how it was seen by a couple in 2015 who reportedly decided to have sex on top of the wall of the historic Vauban Fortress. Unfortunately for the lovers (and for those who found them), they **perished after falling, naked, over 30 feet into the castle moat.** Police suggested to a French newspaper, in the most French way, that this was just a case of lovemaking gone wrong.

"Death is
a delightful
hiding place for
weary men."

—HERODOTUS

**Chapter 3**

# WORKED
# TO DEATH

# Talk about being worked to death.

The modern era is generally one of improvement: faster internet, more medicines, and a broad increase in the storehouse of human knowledge. There are some backward steps, though. For one thing, hair dryers have to come with warning labels. For another, work-related deaths are on the rise. According to the U.S. Bureau of Labor Statistics, **a worker died from a work-related injury every 101 minutes in 2021.** The following year, it was every 96 minutes. And the industries and injuries cover a broad range. Whatever people are doing out there, *stop it.*

# That oil-rig job pays well for a reason.

Between 2008 and 2017, the U.S. oil and gas industry had blowout success, boosting output and hiring new workers as fast as they could. The boom did not lead to extra safety regulations, though. In that stretch, **over 1,500 oil and gas workers died on the job.** To put that into perspective, fewer American soldiers were killed in Afghanistan during that time. Still, the industry insists that extra precautions are unnecessary. When your boss sees workers dying in myriad ways (explosions, vehicle crashes, being burnt alive) and says, "Nothing to see here," it might be time to consider a career change.

> *"I don't want to achieve immortality through my work. I want to achieve it through not dying."*
> —WOODY ALLEN

## Don't take your eyes off the pasta.

Chef Juan Ruiz was working in his Mexico City restaurant one day in 2005 when a surprise storm blasted through the city. Winds peaked at around 150 mph. In conditions like that, most people would worry about flying glass or collapsing roofs. They wouldn't be too concerned about nearby food. **But, in the ensuing chaos, pasta became a deadly projectile.** Ruiz was struck through the heart by strands of uncooked spaghetti, which, at that velocity, had become as deadly as knives. One shudders to think of the damage lasagna noodles would have done.

## Death by discount shopping is a thing.

People go to dollar stores because they can be found just about everywhere, and the products are cheap. But these havens for the frugal shopper are also hiding a dark secret: since 2014, **nearly 50 people have been killed and 172 injured at one of the more popular chains.** Coincidentally (or not), the chain has also been fined repeatedly for workplace safety violations. That doesn't mean people don't need to save a dollar here and there. But one-ply toilet paper and off-brand canned food comes at too high a price for the unlucky few.

## Every so often, the bull gets his revenge.

Bullfighting seems one-sided. The human matador has swords; the bull has nowhere to run. Thousands of ill-fated bulls die this way, but the sheer *possibility* of a matador being on the receiving end of those horns keeps the stands filled. And it turns out that the human loses sometimes. **In 2016, Spanish matador Victor Barrio lost his life in the ring on live TV after being gored through the chest.** While Barrio was the first matador to die in a match since 1985, over thirty others had been killed that way in the previous century by bulls who had clearly had enough of those flapping red capes.

## Oligarchs need better windows.

Post-Soviet Russia presented many opportunities for oligarchs. These high-powered businessmen were known to skirt the law, but if they followed politicians' orders, they were left alone. Then Russia invaded Ukraine again in 2022 and things got weird (when not outright horrific). **Several oligarchs, especially those who criticized the war, started dying in a strangely similar way: falling out of windows.** Ravil Maganov, chairman of oil producer Lukoil, died after plummeting from a Moscow hospital room. Sausage tycoon Pavel Antov died after falling out of a southern India hotel window. Gold-covered mansions and half-billion-dollar yachts are great, but barred windows might be helpful.

# Didn't management tell them about the poison paint?

After being discovered by Marie Curie in 1898, radium was seen as a cool glowing substance, not a danger. In the early twentieth century, thousands of factory workers—most of them female—used radium-heavy paint to make luminous watch dials. **They were told to point their brushes by licking them, thus ingesting small bits of toxic paint.** Later known as the "Radium Girls," many of those workers developed cancer, "radium jaw" (where the radium destroys the bone), and other painful conditions, leading to several deaths. Though people were aware of radium necrosis by the mid-1920s, producers didn't phase out radium paint in watches until 1968. That's a disturbingly long time, no matter how neat it is to see the time in the dark.

# Automation is killing more than jobs.

People worried about the harm that robots could cause even before they existed. But science fiction broke into the real world in 1979. That January, Robert Williams was getting parts from the storage area of a Ford Motors casting plant in Michigan. **The arm of a five-story-tall robot designed to pull parts from the same spot smashed into Williams, killing him instantly.** In 1981, it was Kenji Urada at a Kawasaki plant. And at least forty-one people lost their lives to industrial robots between 1992 and 2017. Despite these shocking fatalities, companies are still introducing powerful robots into every possible industry. So give those food-delivery robots a wide berth.

# Let sleeping soldiers lie.

One night in 1970 on an American base in South Vietnam, Marine Sergeant Richard L. Tate found Private Gary A. Hendricks napping on guard duty. The sergeant berated the private and thought no more of it. That is, until the next night, when the private tossed a fragmentation hand grenade into the sergeant's bunker. **The explosion killed the sergeant and wounded two other officers.** It was one of the war's most infamous cases of "fragging." The private later told psychiatrists he didn't remember anything about it, which, if true, points to something more frightening for discipline-minded officers to consider: sleep-fragging.

# Leave window testing to the professionals.

Have you ever looked at floor-to-ceiling windows and thought, "I could break that"? Of course not. But then, you are not Garry Hoy. A rising lawyer in a Toronto law firm, **Hoy liked to amuse people by throwing himself against an unbreakable window in the firm's twenty-fourth-floor office.** Every time, he bounced off. Until he didn't. Showing off at a party in 1993, Hoy took a run at a window, and it held. Then he pushed his luck and did it again, this time going right through when the glass popped out of its frame. The episode was traumatizing enough that several lawyers quit, proving that, sometimes, giving up is the right answer.

# That's an extremely
# bad day at work.

One of the more curious aspects of modern-day London, England, is the invention known as the telescopic urinal. These are public toilets stored underground that rise up hydraulicly when summoned like some kind of android from *Doctor Who*. This went very poorly for sixty-year-old Kevin Holding, who was **crushed in 2023 underneath a toilet that dropped suddenly** while he was working on it in London's West End. Despite the efforts of a couple dozen firefighters, Holding died from his injuries.

# This wouldn't have happened on the
# set of *Love Actually*.

If there's one thing Hollywood has taught us, it's that if you're making a movie about demonic possession, you should take out extra life insurance. Production on William Friedkin's 1973 vomit-spewing shocker *The Exorcist*, for example, went badly from the start. The set caught on fire. **Crew members lost body parts to accidents (a toe here, a thumb there).** Relatives of actors died. Even actor Jack MacGowran himself died of complications from the flu. All that notwithstanding, co-star Max von Sydow had an appropriately cool Scandinavian take: "If you shoot something for a year, people are going to get hurt; people are going to die."

# Sitting at a desk all day is bad for your health.

William Barclay "Bat" Masterson was just twenty-two years old in 1876, when he had his first shootout. (Bat survived; the other guy didn't.) But what the famed gunslinger/prizefighter/bodyguard/occasional sheriff really wanted to do was write. After moving to New York City, the multitalented Masterson started writing a sports column for the *New York Morning Telegraph*. **He kept that up until the morning of October 25, 1921, when he collapsed of a heart attack at his typewriter.** After a pretty active life, it was the desk job that did him in.

## SURVIVAL TIP

There's a simple solution to the death-by-desk-job phenomenon: literally just get up and move around, ideally every half hour or so. Go bother some of your colleagues and don't feel guilty about it. (They don't want you to die, do they?) Get a glass of water, which will keep you hydrated and ensure that you have to get up again later.

# Chicken is a dangerous business.

Farming is not for the faint of heart, but mass-producing poultry products seems particularly dicey. The Tyson Foods River Valley Animal Foods plant in Arkansas paid a half-million-dollar fine for violating safety regulations after employee Jason Kelley died in 2003 from inhaling hydrogen sulfide gas. In 2009, a more shocking fatality occurred at the same plant. When an unnamed worker in the process of dumping offal got out of his tractor trailer to investigate a malfunctioning tailgate, the tailgate released and swept him into the bin. **He drowned under an avalanche of offal.** And those are just two of several cases to grace accident reports, which is something to think about when weighing career options.

# Turns out, the geese weren't the problem.

Residents of the Chicago suburb of Villa Park really hated geese. They hired a local company to keep the troublesome species away by introducing swans to the area's ponds, with employee Anthony Hensley patrolling the waters as backup. One day in 2012, **Hensley was working a pond in his kayak when he was attacked by angry swans.** He fell into the water and tried to make it to shore, but the birds continued their attack. Sadly, Hensley drowned. Although fatal assaults by these graceful yet aggressive waterfowl are unusual, they are not unknown. The less-appreciated geese, on the other hand, have been connected to approximately zero fatalities.

# Deep breaths save lives.

Jasper "Jack" Newton Daniel opened his Lynchburg, Tennessee, whiskey distillery just after the Civil War. It succeeded, thanks both to the area's limestone-filtered spring water and a country wanting to drink away the past. Despite his triumph, Daniel still had a temper. Unable to get into the office safe one day, Daniel kicked it out of anger and smashed his big toe. **That led to an infection, which led to amputations, which led to Daniel dying of blood poisoning years later in 1911,** which led to you reading about it and thinking, "Maybe I should give that mindfulness thing a try."

# Time to look at jobs in solar power.

It's no surprise that coal mining is not the easiest occupation. Between cave-ins and black-lung disease, it definitely falls into the category of life-threatening jobs. But digging out coal in China appears to be especially deadly. Government statistics (remember, those are probably the *rosier* numbers) are staggering: **over a quarter-million dead coal miners in China, just since 1949.** The industry has improved its safety record over time. In recent years, China was recording 7.29 deaths per million metric tons of coal, compared to only .04 deaths in the United States. (Look at that: America is doing something right for once when it comes to worker safety.)

## Human Resources
## isn't all bad.

Before HR was a thing, it seems like anything went in the workplace. Take George Spencer Millet, for example. The fair-complected blond teenager was an office boy at a New York insurance company. On his fifteenth birthday, in 1909, which just happened to be the day after Valentine's Day, a gang of women from the stenography pool rushed Millet and smothered him in kisses. **The shy Millet scrambled away from the love onslaught and collapsed in a pool of blood.** In all the romantic confusion, a small knife known as an ink eraser, which had been in his shirt pocket, punctured the poor boy's heart.

## Where do big boats go to die,
## and who do they kill?

When large ships are no longer seaworthy or get supplanted by newer models, they are sailed to countries like India and Bangladesh. There, appropriately named shipbreakers break up the massive vessels for scrap in astonishingly dangerous and unregulated conditions. Working with no safety or protective equipment, these workers face severe injuries and shockingly high odds of dying. **In fact, one shipbreaker dies each week** as they cut apart the huge metal hulls with handheld blow torches while dealing with dangerous falls, poisonous chemicals, fires, and explosions. It's the kind of work that puts that one summer you spent at McDonald's into perspective.

# Sometimes, it really is better to ask for permission than for forgiveness.

The crew of *Midnight Rider*, a film about rock legend Gregg Allman, was on their first shoot in 2014 when tragedy struck. The director had moved a dream sequence with star William Hurt to a rickety old railway bridge in Georgia. **When cast and crew heard the howl of a freight train, they had just seconds before it crashed through the impromptu set.** Twenty-seven-year-old camera assistant Sarah Jones didn't make it out of harm's way. When the film's producers hedged about whether they had been granted access for shooting, one of Jones's friends told an industry magazine, "It's not complicated; you either have permission or you don't."

## Talk about a body slam.

One of the standout stars of the 1980s and '90s professional wrestling circuit was Owen Hart. The Canadian wrestled around the world before starting to make it big in American matches. On May 23, 1999, Hart was scheduled for a Kansas City match, costumed as his masked "Blue Blazer" character. **He'd just begun his dramatic entrance from the arena's ceiling when his safety harness malfunctioned, dropping him nearly 80 feet to the mat.** He died minutes later, but the show went on as scheduled. The winner of the evening's fake fighting? Ironically, The Undertaker.

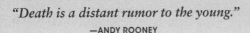
## How extreme is too extreme?

Despite its name, the Winter X (for "extreme") Games managed a good safety record for many years since beginning in 1997. Serious injuries were common, but fatalities were unheard of. That changed in 2013. **Caleb Moore's 450-pound snowmobile landed on top of him during an attempted back flip, giving him a concussion.** (It was his eleventh from the Games.) Just minutes later, his brother Colten Moore had an accident in the very same spot, falling off his snowmobile and separating his pelvis. Though Colten survived, Caleb died days later.

## I vote for not dying.

Voter fraud was once rampant—and deadly. In the United Kingdom, unsavory political bosses got votes the usual way (bribery, intimidation). When that didn't work, they used "cooping" (forcibly plying voters with booze until they agreed to vote for a certain candidate, several times if possible). Eventually, this practice came to America, where it may have done in Edgar Allan Poe. **The writer was found hallucinating near a Baltimore tavern being used as a polling place on Election Day 1849, before expiring several days later.** Election fraud may not be as creepy as his *The Masque of the Red Death*, but apparently, it can be just as deadly.

# A not-so-sweet ending.

Making treats and candies is not the kind of occupation most people think of as dangerous (at least, those who have never read *Charlie and the Chocolate Factory*). But, apparently, there is no such thing as a completely safe job. In December 2016, Svetlana Rosalina, a young worker at the Sergiev-Posad confectionary plant just outside Moscow, **lost her life after plummeting into a mixing vat and being blended with its sugary contents.** It was reported she may have fallen while trying to retrieve her phone, which, if true, means the blame lies squarely with smartphones and not sweets.

# This sort of thing didn't happen at Los Alamos.

In the 1950s, the U.S. Army thought it would be cool to have plug-and-go nuclear reactors they could ship wherever they had remote bases needing dependable power. They built a prototype reactor, the SL-1, at an Idaho facility and started training crews in 1958. Three years later, a meltdown caused a nuclear explosion that killed the unlucky three-man night shift: Richard Leroy McKinley, Jack Byrnes, and Richard Legg. **Legg's body had been pinned to the ceiling by debris, while McKinley's was so radioactive that he had to be buried in a coffin lined with lead.** On the bright side, they are the only known deaths in the United States caused by a nuclear accident to this day.

# That's not what he signed up for.

Up until a few decades ago, it was accepted practice for medical professionals to coerce human test subjects (prisoners, military personnel, asylum inmates, children) into doing dangerous things. In 1953, British researchers studying the effects of nerve gas recruited Royal Air Force personnel for testing, promising safety and 15 shillings a week. With twenty-year-old Ronald Maddison, they failed to hold up their end of the bargain. **The promising young RAF mechanic died of nerve-gas poisoning after its liquid form was applied to his skin.** A secret court of inquiry blamed a "personal idiosyncrasy" in the victim's metabolism. The fact that they changed dosing protocol from 200mg to 5mg afterward was a total coincidence.

# Even good translations can kill.

In the 1520s, Oxford-educated scholar William Tyndale decided that an English translation of the Catholic Church's Latin-only Bible would let Christians decide what to believe without priests acting as biased middlemen. **Making and smuggling those English Bibles got Tyndale arrested. His beliefs got him dead.** (The Church was getting nervous about the rise of Protestantism, you see.) Convicted of heresy in 1536, Tyndale was tied to a stake, where he was strangled to death before his body was burned for good measure. Apparently, the executioners had not read all those translated verses about forgiveness.

# No one said space travel was safe.

A lot can go wrong when you're an astronaut (or cosmonaut). This was all too apparent in 1967. That April, Soviet test pilot Vladimir Komarov blasted into orbit in the *Soyuz 1*. The craft's mechanical issues, combined with the January 1967 *Apollo 1* tragedy, in which three American astronauts burned to death on the launchpad, had everyone on edge. But Moscow was pushing, so up Komarov went. **On reentry, the parachutes malfunctioned, and Komarov hurtled to his death.** According to the Soviet transcripts, among his last words transmitted were, "I feel excellent; everything's in order."

# Look out for falling art.

You've probably seen your share of Richard Serra sculptures. His pieces have adorned many American downtowns, public spaces, and museums over the years. While fascinating, these hulking and often rusty slabs of metal are also occasionally quite dangerous. Serra's evocatively titled "Sculpture No. 3"—a pair of 5-ton steel plates propped against each other—was being installed at Minneapolis's Walker Art Center in 1971 when **one of the giant plates fell on and killed worker Raymond Johnson.** *Artforum* memorably (and a bit morbidly) described the moment as "art having an 'impact' on the public."

# Meteorology, but make it extreme.

For the first part of the twentieth century, U.S. weather forecasters were prohibited from saying "tornado." Meteorologists couldn't predict tornadoes, so broadcasters felt such announcements would spread panic for no reason. The daring pursuit of better warning systems by "storm chasers" (think the movie *Twister*) and improvements in technology changed that, but at a cost. The first three chasers to pay it were Tim Samaras, his son Paul Samaras, and Carl Young. While chasing a devastating Oklahoma twister, **the storm's high-speed winds grabbed and smashed their car.** Before his tragic death, Tim, who would record detailed storm videos during his pursuits, was known as "the guy who always gets the killer shot."

## SURVIVAL TIP

You wouldn't chase a forest fire, so don't chase tornadoes, no matter how cool they look. And definitely don't stand on your porch and record one coming your way. Go to your basement. If that's not an option, hunker down under a thick blanket in an inside room, hallway, or closet without windows. Also keep in mind what's above you—if the ceiling gives, that refrigerator could come crashing down on you.

# Stay put.

You might think that jobs where violence is part of the terrain, like police officer or prison guard, are the most dangerous occupations. Not true. Even firefighters don't take the top spot. What kind of jobs are most likely to be your last (and not because you retired with a gold watch)? According to a 2023 U.S. Department of Labor report, those would be the "transportation and material moving occupations," which include railroad worker, truck driver, air traffic controller, and flight attendant. **Workers in that category suffered 1,620 fatal work injuries in 2022,** more than any other occupational group. (That desk job is suddenly sounding more appealing.)

# Killed in the colored smoke of war.

As euphemisms go, "friendly fire" is one of the most divorced from reality. It describes when soldiers mistakenly attack their own, and it's an unfortunately common occurrence in the confusion of combat. One of more egregious modern examples was Operation Cobra, the Allies' 1944 post-D-Day offensive. **A massive bombing and artillery assault meant to pulverize the German front lines ended up also killing 111 American troops.** And it all came down to a breeze that moved colored smoke meant to mark German positions over American lines.

## "People before profits," said no oil company ever.

The *Deepwater Horizon* was a massive, half-billion-dollar, semi-submersible oil-drilling platform designed, as the name implies, for extremely deep waters. It was drilling in the Gulf of Mexico on April 20, 2010, when a blowout started a fire that ripped across the vessel. **The crew had only minutes to escape; 11 out of 126 died.** Investigations determined the tragedy was partially caused by the operating companies' mistakes and shortcuts. While the explosion happened fast, the aftermath lingered in the form of the largest U.S. oil spill ever and a toxic legacy in the Gulf that likely caused many more deaths.

## That was some fastball.

Many words come to mind when thinking of baseball, but "deadly" isn't one of them. As of printing, only one player has ever died while playing America's pastime (but there's still time). During an August 1920 pennant game between the New York Yankees and Cleveland Indians, **a Yankees brushback pitch cracked Indians shortstop Ray Chapman in the head.** Chapman made it to the hospital but died after surgery. One theory for why he didn't move out of the ball's trajectory is that he couldn't see it. Back then, pitchers covered balls in everything from dirt to chew to improve their grip. Chapman's death put a bad spin on these so-called "spitballs," which were subsequently banned.

> *"There is nothing safer than flying—*
> *it's crashing that is dangerous."*
> **—THEO COWAN**

## No good deed . . .

Roberto Clemente's hero status is difficult to overstate. One of the greatest baseball players of all time, Puerto Rican–born Clemente overcame significant discrimination after making his professional debut in 1955. He was also a dedicated humanitarian. And on the last day of 1972, **just months after making his 3,000th hit, he met a hero's end.** Clemente was delivering much-needed relief to earthquake-ravaged Nicaragua when his cargo plane plunged into the Atlantic Ocean.

## Even a tennis ball can pack a deadly punch.

You would not expect a genteel sport like tennis to be risky. But, once again, there is always reason for concern, especially in a sport where tennis balls have been clocked at over 100 mph. During a boys' singles match at the U.S. Open in 1983, **Sweden's Stefan Edberg hit a serve right into the groin of linesman Richard Wertheim.** The force of the blow knocked Wertheim back, causing his chair to tip over and his head to hit the hard surface. Wertheim died from internal cranial bleeding. (If there's any justice in the world, the head injury kept the poor guy from feeling the pain of the hit itself.)

# Watch your back—and neck— at the ice rink.

Hockey is known as a violent sport, probably because of its tradition of players using body checks, hockey sticks, or just their fists to fight on the ice. But there are less obvious perils. In December 2023, the International Ice Hockey Federation announced they would require neck guards for all players who are not adults. **This was after two players died in two years from being cut on the neck by another player's skate**—hockey pro Adam Johnson and high school sophomore Teddy Balkind. The new rule is great for the pros but not much comfort for anyone else who enjoys an ice rink and has to skate guard-less.

# The (last) performance of a lifetime.

Opera demands a lot from its performers, who often strain to hit the high and sustained notes in an aria. Talented tenor Richard Versalle died from the effort. In January 1996, Versalle was playing a law clerk in Leoš Janáček's *The Makropulos Case* at New York's Metropolitan Opera. **He had just climbed up a 10-foot-tall sliding ladder for the opening scene when he was hit by a fatal heart attack and fell to the stage.** Ironically, the last words the sixty-three-year-old sang were, "Too bad you can only live so long."

# And for my next act—
# a heart attack.

Standup isn't for the faint of heart either. In 1987, actor and comedian Dick Shawn was workshopping new gags for 500 San Diegans. Not long after a routine in which he played a politician who declared, "I will not lay down on the job," Shawn fell on his face. **The audience, knowing Shawn's predilection for unusual comic bits, assumed it was a joke.** It was a fatal heart attack. A few doctors in the crowd tried reviving him, but to no avail. By the time Shawn was declared dead in the ambulance, many audience members had left, thinking they had just witnessed a great, if bizarre, piece of alternative comedy.

# They died for his art.

Christo was famous for his massive art installations that were way too big for museums, and in 1991, he also became infamous. That was the year he and his wife, Jeanne-Claude, installed their *The Umbrellas* project: thousands of bright yellow and blue umbrellas scattered over one valley in California and another in Japan. That sounds harmless enough, until you learn that **each one stood 20 feet high and 28 feet wide and weighed 488 pounds.** The $26 million project came to an end after one umbrella in California blew over and crushed a woman to death against a boulder. Adding injury to injury, an unfortunate crane operator who was dismantling the Japanese umbrellas accidentally hit a power line and was fatally electrocuted.

# It wasn't the kind of armored-car death you'd expect.

Armored-car guards naturally worry about possible robberies, but Hrand Arakelian's death unlocked a new fear for the industry. On February 4, 1986, his partner, Scott Daniel Bauman, slammed on the brakes to avoid hitting a swerving car. **The sudden deceleration caused $50,000 worth of 25-pound boxes of quarters to fall on Arakelian.** In his haste to find help for Arakelian, Bauman locked his keys inside the truck. By the time a locksmith and paramedics arrived, Arakelian was dead.

# Going down?

Odds are good that you will not be killed by an elevator. According to one manufacturer, its elevators carry as many people as currently live on the Earth every five days. How many of those passengers die? That's harder to find out, but the consensus seems to be around a couple dozen a year. **A few of those deaths involve rectangular metal canisters full of humans flying down narrow shafts at high rates of speed.** But many are the result of natural causes and bad timing. Still, most elevator-related deaths involve people who are paid to work on them, which is something to remember during that job hunt.

# That's not what human composting is.

One of the most gruesome work-related ways to die has to be via woodchipper. Woodchippers are big, growling machines that consume everything from branches to entire trees, using dizzyingly fast steel blades, and shoot them out the other end as tiny wood chips or mulch. **Every so often, somebody falls (or gets yanked into) one of these terrifying machines and, well, you can guess the rest.** Forty-one people died that way between 1982 and 2016. Most of those deaths were accidental, but a good rule of thumb is to never pick a fight with someone who works in horticulture.

## SURVIVAL TIP

What's the best way not to die when handling trees (besides not being anywhere near a woodchipper)? Tight clothes, no jewelry, and a lot of mindfulness. And if you've never handled a chainsaw or other landscaping machinery before, don't. Call a pro.

# You don't want to get pinned by the pinsetter.

You might think that bowling balls are the most dangerous thing at a bowling alley. After all, they usually weigh about 15 pounds and are hurled toward faraway targets by people a couple beers in. But most bowling-related fatalities involve pinsetters, the machines that replace the pins after they have been knocked down. In one such instance in 2018, the sixty-five-year-old owner of a Colorado bowling alley, Ector Rodriguez, was trying to fix his automatic pinsetter when he was **impaled by the machine.** Sadly, there are plenty of other examples, too, but one is awful enough to keep you away from pinsetters for life.

# A carpet is more than just a tripping hazard.

Owning a small business has its surprises, which usually involve things like stiff competition or having trouble with taxes but can occasionally include death. In 2009, an unnamed partner in a flooring store in Mesa, Arizona, had not been at work long when **a thousand-pound roll of carpet fell and trapped him underneath.** Somebody tried to use a forklift to get the carpet off him, but he was already dead. And he wasn't the first. Warehouse worker Ignacio Reed met a similar fate in Santa Ana, California, in 1998. If it's any consolation, statistics say you're far more likely to die from tripping over carpet than from being crushed by it.

# Turf wars over ice-cream trucks were a real thing.

The bleak housing projects built outside Glasgow in the 1970s were so isolated that ice-cream vans branched out into selling everything from toilet paper to drugs. Then gangsters stepped in and started violent turf battles. At the peak of these so-called "ice-cream wars" in 1984, an eighteen-year-old driver named Andrew Doyle was being threatened to give up his route. When he didn't relent, **he and five members of his family were killed in an arson attack.** Twenty years later, the men jailed for the crime won an appeal by implicating the police. So that's sure to make everyone in the area feel safer.

# This is why you need adequate training to handle uranium.

On September 30, 1999, three workers at the Tokaimura nuclear fuel-processing plant in Japan were making fuel rods. While pouring enriched uranium oxide into a bucket, they inadvertently bypassed a safeguard that would have prevented them from using too much. They were concerned when they noticed a flash of blue light, the first indication that **they had accidentally started a nuclear chain reaction.** Although the accident was mostly contained, Hisashi Ouchi, who had been closest to the uranium, was critically injured. Reports said he was exposed to more radiation than anybody in history. It was an unwanted distinction, leading as it did to a months-long agonizing death from radiation poisoning.

"Extinction
is the rule.
Survival is the
exception."

—CARL SAGAN

**Chapter 4**

# WHEN ANIMALS ATTACK

# Killed by small dogs: painful *and* embarrassing.

The odds of being killed by a Dachshund are low, which is reassuring—but never say never! In May 2018, fifty-two-year-old Tracy Garcia was outside her home near Ardmore, Oklahoma, when the poor woman was swarmed by seven small yet extremely vicious dogs. The dogs were reportedly **a flea-bitten pack of young Dachshund–terrier mixes, weighing less than forty pounds each,** who belonged to a neighbor. Garcia died shortly after the mauling.

# Feed. The. Sheep.

In 1999, a woman in Durhan, England, was riding around her property on an ATV with a bale of hay strapped to the back. This enraged a flock of some sixty-odd sheep, who hadn't had much grass to eat due to it being winter. **The peckish sheep charged the woman.** Trying to get at the hay, they leapt onto the ATV, sending sixty-seven-year-old Betty Stobbs over a 100-foot cliff and into a quarry. Though she might have survived the fall, the ATV followed her down and landed on top of the poor woman. Stobbs's loyal sheepdog survived the plunge and was found guarding her body (possibly while plotting revenge against her killers).

# Asian rice farmers and deadly snakes need each other—sort of.

The Russell's viper (*Daboia russelii*) is one of the world's nastier snakes. Distributed from Pakistan to Bangladesh, they can grow to more than five feet long and have scary-big fangs. They are particularly common in rice paddies, where they provide some benefit for the human farmers by hunting rodent pests. At the same time, they are **aggressive even on a good day and deliver a deadly wallop of venom.** Effects of a bite include spontaneous hemorrhaging, bleeding from the gums, and acute renal failure. Also worrisome: People who think they've survived a Russell's viper bite can then show symptoms weeks later.

# Don't annoy the viper.

If you are in drier regions just above the equator in Africa, Arabia, and southern Asia, you may see a saw-scaled viper. These snakes grow to up to about three feet long and **kill more people every year than all other snakes combined.** Their venom is not the most toxic; in fact, it causes death less than 10 percent of the time when victims are untreated. What makes the saw-scaled viper so dangerous is their sheer irritability, combativeness, and lightning-fast strike. Even less-deadly venom becomes a problem after multiple bites from a creature that is really uninterested in listening to reason.

# Just let the bear
# have a drink.

In 1891 in Vilnius (then Russia, now Lithuania), tavern owner
Isaack Rabbanovitch faced a dilemma. He was disturbed one day
when a bear came into his business and tried to take a keg of
vodka. Rather than doing what most would have done ("Vodka?
All yours, Mister or Missus Bear!"), Rabbanovitch chose to fight
for his liquor. It didn't go his way. Locals later **found the bear
drunk and asleep on the tavern floor,** with the bodies of
Rabbanovitch and three of his children nearby.

## SURVIVAL TIP

If you find yourself in the vicinity of a bear, try
to stay calm—at least outwardly. Screaming
or running away is far more likely to get you
killed. Talk to the bear so it knows you're
human. Make lots of noise and make yourself
look as big as possible (wave your arms like a
maniac; it beats being mauled) before slowly
moving away. And if you're attacked, remember this
saying: "If it's brown, lie down; if it's black, fight back."

# Being trampled to death is just part of the attraction.

Every year, crowds of people run down twisting alleys with a herd of rampaging bulls close behind. These "bull runnings" happen in various Spanish towns, and some human participants fare better than others. (Bulls can weigh up to 1,500 pounds, which is a lot of kinetic energy when colliding with a human.) At least fifteen people have died since 1924 at the famous annual bull running in Pamplona. In 2016, a man in the Valencia village of Pedreguer was **gored to death by a bull while trying to help another injured runner** during a fiesta. According to one article about the tragedy, "The town suspended all bull-related festivities for the rest of the day."

# Flying tortoises are more than the stuff of video games.

Legend has it that the Greek dramatist Aeschylus was sitting by the water, minding his own business, one day around 455 BCE. Suddenly, a passing eagle looking for a rock on which to smash a tortoise noticed the man's bald head and decided, "This will do." **One high-velocity reptile later, and the great Aeschylus was no more.** However, had he known the manner of his demise, the playwright likely would have been sanguine about it. He once wrote, "For it would be better to die once and for all than to suffer pain for all one's life."

# If there are owls around, wear a helmet.

When Kathleen Peterson was found dead in the Durham, North Carolina, home she shared with her husband Michael in 2001, suspicion fell on him. He was found guilty of murder after a high-profile trial (although a new trial in 2011 downgraded the charge to manslaughter). A different theory was later raised: **What if Kathleen was murdered by a bird?** Scalp wounds and a feather in her hair indicated she could have been attacked by a barred owl. This, combined with her being intoxicated on wine and pills, could have caused her to fall down the staircase where her body was discovered. Barred owls have been known to attack hikers who come across their path, and one accidentally trapped inside a house might have been particularly aggressive. Unfortunately for Michael, no owls have come forward.

# Even flightless birds can get you.

Country legend Johnny Cash once had his own exotic animal reserve. He was often harassed by an angry ostrich named Waldo while walking through the reserve. (Ostriches, by the way, can stand 9 feet tall and weigh 350 pounds.) Things got so dicey one time in 1981 that Cash swung a stick at Waldo, who came back at him with a favorite ostrich tactic: **disemboweling a target with a vicious slashing kick from one of their massive talons.** Cash later wrote that he "got off lightly" because of his big belt buckle, with some deep cuts to his stomach and a couple broken ribs. Unfortunately, Cash never recorded a song about the incident.

# Very cute yet very, very deadly.

A pesky truth is that the animals people are most frightened of (lions, for example) are not actually the most dangerous. The large mammal that causes the most human fatalities turns out to be the hippopotamus. These massive (3,000 pounds and up) semi-amphibious creatures, found in sub-Saharan Africa, like to hang out in the water, munching on grass, until a boat full of unsuspecting humans comes by. Then those boaters get a good look at **the territorial creature's massive canines and gaping mouths.** About 500 people die from hippo attacks each year.

## That cuddle with your cat might be your last.

The Steere House Nursing and Rehabilitation Center in Providence, Rhode Island, stood out from other nursing homes for a delightful reason: Its operators had adopted a half-dozen cats to provide comfort, even to the dog people. One cat was special, though. Usually standoffish, Oscar occasionally curled up with patients. It was pointed out that many, if not all of, **the patients he snuggled up with died soon afterward.** Oscar's predictive abilities proved so accurate that staff would call the patients' families to say their goodbyes once the cat had settled in with them. Scientists think felines may be able to detect subtle pre-mortem chemical changes, but cat lovers argue they just know when they're needed.

# It's still a bear.

Viewers of Werner Herzog's 2005 documentary *Grizzly Man* will never forget what happened: Bear fan Timothy Treadwell spent multiple summers filming himself hanging out with ursines in Alaska's Katmai National Park. **He became convinced he had a special bond with the bears.** During a 2001 interview with David Letterman, the talk show host joked that Treadwell would be eaten by a bear. In October 2003, Treadwell and girlfriend Amie Huguenard were killed and, indeed, partially eaten by a bear. Treadwell's last words were caught on tape, among them: "I'm getting killed."

# This kiss you will regret.

Itchy at night? That scratch might kill you. Triatomine bugs are nasty bloodsuckers with a cute nickname: "kissing bugs." They are concentrated in the Americas, where they creep around at night and attach themselves to sleeping people's faces. Once locked in, they **suck as much blood as they can get**— hence, the name. A more appropriate nickname would be "assassin bugs." That's because, while sucking blood, they also drop tiny feces that often contain a parasite that causes Chagas disease. Then people inadvertently infect themselves by scratching their bites. While not always fatal, about 14,000 people a year die from Chagas, which, in its chronic phase, can affect the heart.

# Bad monkeys—bad!

In 2007, the deputy mayor S. Singh Bajwa of New Delhi, India, was faced with an unusual problem: his house was being attacked by rhesus monkeys. **While trying to curb the aggressive creatures swarming over his home's terrace, Bajwa fell to the street.** He died from serious head wounds. The city's residents may be fed up with such attacks from the small and cute but fatally irritating primates, but according to Hindu tradition, they cannot be hunted or harmed. Ahead of the G20 summit in 2023, New Delhi officials came up with a way to minimize their mischief: they put up life-size cutouts of larger langur monkeys to ever so gently ward off their smaller counterparts.

# They could kill you . . . eventually.

Conservationists like to say nice things about the animals they want to protect. That's difficult when it comes to the slow loris. Though they are the cutest-looking creatures you'll see in the Indonesian jungle, slow lorises are bitey little things who **deliver flesh-rotting venom with their sharp canines.** The tiny, giant-eyed primates were described by conservationist Anna Nekaris as "if the killer bunnies on *Monty Python* were a real animal." Others have called slow lorises "venomous furballs of death." There is no record of any humans' faces rotting off because of a slow loris bite. But give them time.

# The aquarium is
# probably safer.

The Smithsonian's National Zoo in Washington, D.C., is a national treasure, with over 400 species represented on its 163-acre campus. It is also, on occasion, somewhat deadly. The lions are among the most dangerous inhabitants, having mauled a young girl to death in 1958 as well as a mentally ill woman who snuck into their enclosure in 1995. But other animals have proved their fearsomeness, as well—like **the Gaboon vipers who bit and nearly killed the teenager** who tried stealing them from the zoo in 1983. (Those fences are there for a reason, people.)

# Call it a hog, swine, or pig:
# it's deadly.

Large Eurasian boars imported to American game reserves later broke free and bred with smaller domesticated pigs to create something fearsome: the feral swine. This wide-ranging, mean-tempered, and hard-to-kill pest **weighs up to 400 pounds and is now swarming by the millions across the southern United States**. The invasive creatures cause billions of dollars in damage annually and even kill people, like healthcare worker Christine Marie Rollins, who died after being attacked by multiple feral swine when she was visiting a patient near Houston, Texas, in 2019. If that isn't worrisome enough, nobody seems to have any ideas for how to manage what one government report unforgettably termed the "Feral Swine Bomb."

> *"Death is nature's way of saying,*
> *'Your table is ready.'"*
> **—ROBIN WILLIAMS**

## That sting is not just a sting.

If you read enough about mosquitos, you would not want to leave
the house unless you're wearing a hazmat suit. Swatting them away
and getting stung while sitting by a lake is bad enough. Worse?
The diseases that come with the sting. According to Timothy
Winegard's *The Mosquito: A Human History of Our Deadliest
Predator*, **about half of the 108 billion humans who ever
lived have been killed by mosquito-borne illnesses.**
So maybe invest in a few more citronella candles this summer.

## Stay out of the water
## in Florida.

Is it reasonable to assume that every body of water in Florida
contains an alligator that very much wants to eat you? Absolutely.
The only real question is whether the best response is to avoid
Florida lakes and ponds or simply relocate to an alligator-free
state. The Florida Fish and Wildlife Conservation Commission
tries to pooh-pooh all the large-aquatic-lizard worry, saying only
**thirty people have died from unprovoked alligator
bites since 1948**. The fact that the commission defines these
bites as just the "unprovoked" ones makes you wonder how many
people are out there provoking alligators? And why?

## Admire these little guys
## from a distance.

One of the ocean's rarest and most beautiful creatures is the
blue-ringed octopus. These tiny golf ball–size beauties, with
their bright yellow skin covered in flaring blue rings, look
like something dreamed up by the animators of *SpongeBob
SquarePants*. Pretty or not, you do not want to make them angry
or scared. (You can tell because their blue rings brighten.) And
you definitely do not want to touch them. When agitated, this
octopus tends to sting, which injects the offending person with
venom that's **a thousand times deadlier than cyanide.**
And there is no antivenom for these guys. So, back away slowly.

## Nobody ever warns you
## about elk.

In November 2023, a woman was discovered badly injured
outside her Arizona home after having apparently been trampled
by an elk. A bucket of spilled corn was found nearby, suggesting
**she had been trying to feed the elk.** She died days later.
Her death was described by the Game and Fish Department as the
state's "first fatal elk attack." Given that bull elks average around
5 feet tall at the shoulder, can weigh over 1,000 pounds, and use
their antlers as head-mounted spears, feeding them corn or
anything by hand is strongly discouraged.

# What's scarier: great whites or New Yorkers?

Nobody wants to get in the water if they think there is a shark nearby. But everybody wants to go to New York. Why is this relevant? Because, though being chomped on by a prehistoric eating machine is terrifying, getting gnawed on by another person is not enticing, either. Fun(ish) fact: In 1987, thirteen Americans reported shark bites. That same year, **over 1,500 people were bitten by residents of New York City.** Yes, the pizza is good, but maybe it's not worth the risk of a bite from the most unpredictable of animals: the human being.

# Death by python is both painful and weird.

The biggest danger from snakes is usually their venom. That is not the case with reticulated pythons. Native to South and Southeast Asia, these slithery predators grow up to 25 feet long and hunt their prey—which is often large and does include humans—by biting it first, then **quickly wrapping themselves around it to cut off airways and blood circulation.** This leads to a rather surprising and unpleasant, though somewhat rapid, death. Because these pythons can digest every part of a person, it's hard to know how many they've killed.

# Don't blame the pit bull.

There are many differences between having dogs and cats as pets—having to walk the former in the freezing cold, for one. But one of the more crucial things separating the species is that, every so often, one kills people. **Up to fifty people die each year from dog attacks.** But don't be too quick to blame the breeds. Dogs aren't inherently murderous. Those bites are usually the result of human beings creating a dangerous situation through ignorance, neglect, or even intentional training. So who's the real killer: the dog that attacked, or the human who trained him to do it?

# Stay inside the submarine.

When people find themselves a thousand or so feet underwater in the ocean's darkest depths, they are advised to stay inside the pressurized submersible that brought them down there. For one thing, the pressure at that depth would crush a human body like an empty soda can under a boot. But another terrifying prospect is the presence of *Osedax*, aka "zombie worms." These creepy 1- to 3-inch creatures **feed on corpses that have floated down to the deep,** secreting an acid that dissolves bones and allows them to feed on the fat contained within. They usually eat whale carcasses, but they are still nightmare fuel for humans.

# Hitchcock couldn't have predicted it.

Not all bird attacks are intentional. Sometimes they're just the result of two objects occupying the same space. Consider Alan Stacey. An up-and-coming British F1 driver, Stacey raced his first Grand Prix in 1958. Stacey was racing the 1960 Belgian Grand Prix when **a bird smashed into his windshield as he approached a turn at about 120 miles per hour.** This caused him to lose control of the car, which raced up an embankment and punched through a ten-foot-thick hedge before landing in a field, causing his demise at only twenty-six years old.

# This is why doctors recommend a varied diet.

Kings get to eat what kings want to eat. If a monarch decides he wants to live on Big Macs alone, then the staff needs to know the quickest route to the nearest McDonald's drive-thru. In the case of England's Henry I, he had an obsessive love of the squirmy, eel-like, suction-mouthed lamprey. While visiting his hunting lodge in Normandy in 1135, **the king demanded a massive feast of the parasitic fish.** Whether because of overeating or the toxic fish's impact on his insides, Henry went into convulsions and died soon after. The official cause of death? "A surfeit of lampreys."

## Sometimes the animals work together.

South Africa's Kruger National Park is a sprawling game preserve filled with a rich array of iconic animals, from wildebeests to giraffes, cheetahs, and rhinos. That last creature has been a frequent target of poachers over the years, but some of the park's other residents have struck back. In 2019, **park rangers discovered a skull and a pair of pants,** remnants of a suspected rhino poacher. He had been trampled by an elephant before being eaten by a pride of lions, which one might consider fittingly poetic.

## This one time, a dog may have been man's worst friend.

Joseph Smith, a thirty-year-old Kansan, was out hunting with a friend in January 2023 when he was killed in a surprising way. Smith was in the passenger seat of a car his friend was driving. A loaded hunting rifle was on the back seat, as was the friend's German shepherd. When the dog stepped on the rifle's trigger, **a bullet blew through the seat into Smith's back.** Wellington Fire and EMS Chief Timothy Hay didn't blame the dog. Instead, he frankly told a reporter it was a bad idea to leave loaded guns in cars. "At least have the safety on," he advised.

# Know your bees.

In 1956, somebody had the great idea to import a few colonies of African honeybees to Brazil to boost honey production. The following year, twenty-six African honeybee queens and swarms of European honeybee workers escaped from an experimental apiary and started breeding and moving north. This was a problem because the African variant had earned a nickname: "killer bees." **Extremely aggressive and more likely to swarm victims in massive numbers** than their European cousins, Africanized bees have killed roughly a thousand people since coming to the Americas. By all accounts, though, their honey is still delicious.

## SURVIVAL TIP

Most bees have a live-and-let-live philosophy. Just keep your distance and everyone's happy. If you do accidentally incur their wrath, cover your head and run in a straight line to the nearest car or shed. But don't bother hiding in a body of water. The bees can and will wait you out, no matter how long you think you can hold your breath.

# Monkeys only *look* cute.

On October 25, 1920, the world was hit by tragic news: King Alexander of Greece was dead at the age of twenty-seven. Earlier in the month, his dog was attacked by a servant's pet Barbary macaque monkey. While trying to separate the two, Alexander was bitten by yet another monkey. *The New York Times* reported that **the king had been "badly mutilated" in the simian attack**. Although his wounds were cleaned, they were not cauterized, and infection set in. Alexander's death led to a succession crisis, instability, and ultimately the loss of the Greco-Turkish war. Not that the monkeys could have known that would happen.

# Pesticides kill more than just bugs.

Bedbugs have not been directly related to any human fatalities (which is good, because they are bad enough as it is). However, in at least one case, they have been indirectly related to a tragedy. A married couple in their sixties from Lancashire, England, was on vacation in Egypt in 2018 when **they were discovered dead in their hotel bed.** The room next door was being fumigated for bedbugs using the pesticide Lambda, which contained dichloromethane. It seeped into John and Susan Cooper's room and caused carbon monoxide poisoning while they slept.

# Wash your hands.
# Maybe twice.

Most people think nothing of scooping their cat's litter box and then (hopefully) washing their hands. This is just good hygiene, even when there's a scoop between you and anything off-putting. But it is extra urgent due to the *Toxoplasma gondii* parasite, which can be passed from cat feces to humans. Experts believe roughly 60 million Americans are already infected with toxoplasmosis. Most will never have symptoms. But it's especially dangerous for pregnant women and immunocompromised people, **killing roughly 750 people a year.** Of course, cats aren't the only cause—about half those infections are the result of eating undercooked meat. So, don't eat like a cat either.

# Bats are the least
# of your worries.

If you've been nursing a fear of bats, you can rest easier. But think twice about petting any prickly strays on vacation. Rabies, the viral disease often associated with bats, is transmitted through saliva from an infected animal biting you. Although you can get it from bats—as well as from coyotes, raccoons, foxes, and skunks— **the most likely rabies vector is a dog.** A rabid dog is often extremely aggressive, which can make avoiding a bite hard to do. Rabies vaccines are available but not evenly distributed around the world. That is why, of the nearly 60,000 people who die from rabies annually, only one or two are Americans.

# Stay out of the woods.

Ticks are less noticeable than mosquitoes, but they still carry a bioweapons-lab-full of illnesses, from Lyme disease to Rocky Mountain spotted fever. And these tiny, bloodsucking parasites crawl, unnoticed, on you rather than buzzing obnoxiously in your ear. In 2023, Maine reported a death from the little-known tick-borne Powassan virus, severe cases of which can **cause brain inflammation and end in death about 10 percent of the time.** Only about twenty-five people a year catch Powassan in the United States, but it's still one of many good reasons to check for ticks after a walk in the woods.

# Pack your bug spray.

According to one safari expert, an average of one safari tourist dies each year from an animal attack. There is no guarantee the safari you take will not be a fatal one. Trampled by elephants, gored by rhinos, snatched by a leopard—it has all happened. But one slightly more horrifying consideration is that rampaging mammals are less of a threat than the humble mosquito. In Africa, **these little pests have an arsenal of killer diseases they can spread:** Zika, dengue fever, and that old standby, malaria, for example. In fact, they have been deemed "the world's deadliest animal," killing more than 700,000 people each year.

# Well, it certainly wasn't human.

In 1764, the remote mountainous region of Gévaudan, France, was under attack. People were being viciously killed by **a ravening wolf-like monster that often tore its victims' throats out.** Despite military intervention and a 30,000-man posse, the "Beast of Gévaudan" kept up its murderous onslaught, targeting mostly women and children. By the time it was said to have been killed in 1767, the beast had claimed almost a hundred victims. Later theories that the killer was not a monster, but instead a whole pack of wolves or even a cunning human serial killer, do not make the tale any less terrifying.

# No snakes on this plane, but . . .

Most airplane passengers do not wonder, "Hey, does that guy have a crocodile in his duffel bag?" But a horrific story from 2010 suggests they might want to. A passenger on a flight in the Democratic Republic of Congo had packed a crocodile with the intent of selling it. **The animal had different ideas.** It wriggled out of the duffel bag, causing panic as twenty passengers ran to the front of the small plane. That unbalanced the aircraft, which crashed into a house, killing all but one person on board. The crocodile reportedly survived, too.

> *"Crocodiles are easy. They try to kill and eat you. People are harder. Sometimes they pretend to be your friend first."*
> —STEVE IRWIN

## It wasn't a crocodile.

Steve Irwin was a dedicated conservationist who spent a lot of time wrestling crocodiles. That was part of his gig hosting shows like *Crocodile Hunter*, where he got up close and personal with often-frightening animals. The animal that ended his life, though, is known for only attacking if a swimmer steps on it. Filming a segment for his new show, *Ocean's Deadliest*, at Australia's Batt Reef in 2006, Irwin swam up to a stingray. Possibly mistaking him for a dangerous tiger shark, **the animal suddenly stabbed Irwin with the poisonous barb on its tail.** The last thing Irwin did was pull the barb out, but it was too late.

## People are tasty.

For centuries, Arab slave caravans destined for Mombasa passed through the Tsavo savannah (today's southern Kenya). Many enslaved people died, and their bodies were left behind. One theory is that **these people were eaten by the region's lions,** which gave the great cat a taste for humans. A pair of those lions had good hunting in 1898, attacking crews in the Tsavo who were building a railroad bridge. Before the lions were shot and stuffed, they devoured anywhere from 24 to 135 workers. But don't worry: the bridge was finished by early 1899.

# It's their ocean—you're
# just swimming in it.

Jellyfish are some of the most ethereal-looking sea creatures. They are also, because of their ghostly see-through bodies, easy to overlook. That's not great, because jellyfish stings are extremely painful. They are also, on occasion, quite deadly. These seemingly peaceful creatures shoot venom into your body from stingers on their tentacles. The most dangerous among them is the Australian box jellyfish, found off northern Australia and throughout the Indo-Pacific. **Its venom can cause sudden death by paralyzing your lungs and heart.** *Most* of the deaths attributed to them have been between October and May, so just stick to the hotel pool in those months.

# Give the camel his Coke and
# no one gets hurt.

Camels are some of the most ubiquitous domesticated animals. Long used as reliable pack animals across Africa and the Middle East, they are large and sturdy, standing 5 or 6 feet tall and often weighing over 1,000 pounds. They can also be ornery, as people often find out the hard way. **Multiple people have been killed by rampaging camels in the twenty-first century.** Among them was Richard Mileski, the owner of a Tulum, Mexico, wildlife park. In 2015, Mileski was fatally kicked, bitten, and sat on by a camel. One account said that the animal was used to being treated to a Coca-Cola each day, and on the day he didn't get it, he launched his attack.

# "Nature's creative power is far beyond man's instinct of destruction."

—JULES VERNE

## Chapter 5

# THE EARTH HAS IT IN FOR YOU

# Would you rather be killed by aliens, a Yeti, the weather, or your friends?

In January 1959, nine young Soviets set out for a skiing expedition in the Ural Mountains. They never returned. Several weeks later, their bodies were discovered along the slopes of Otorten—which translates to "don't go there" in the language of the Indigenous Mansi people. **Their tent had been slashed open from the inside, and many of the corpses showed brutal wounds, like broken bones and a missing tongue.** The so-called "Dyatlov Pass incident" became one of Russia's most enduring conspiracy theories, with everything from UFOs to Yetis to fellow skiers being blamed. But the real culprit was likely a sudden catastrophic avalanche—an answer that both disappoints conspiracy theorists and is still not particularly comforting to the rest of us.

# Nature always wins.

In 2024, the body of a Japanese man was discovered near the Crystal Cascades waterfall in Queensland, Australia. **He had leaped off a high ledge into the water and never came up.** His death was tragic, as were the deaths of at least three other swimmers in the same area. But no-swimming signs have been posted by the dangerous part of the waterfall for years. Between the twisting waters and the rocks, branches, and pockets beneath it, it's all too easy to drown. That's why nearby Babinda Boulders changed their signage to a list of people who've died. So far, it seems to be working.

# Lava can get you even after it's gone.

When Mauna Loa volcano on Hawaii's Big Island started erupting in 1880, it was a slow-motion catastrophe. After residents did all they could—from building walls to digging a moat to making offerings to Pele, the mythological creator of Hawaii—the town of Hilo was saved. But Mauna Loa kept causing grief. The eruption had created "lava tubes," which is what happens after **lava pouring downhill hardens into natural pipes** through which new lava and water keep flowing. In 2019, seventy-one-year-old Robert Hisashi Nishimoto died after falling into a hidden lava tube while gardening at his house on the Big Island. The police report stated that no foul play was suspected, which lets the volcano off easy.

# Did you feel that?

Seismologists generally know *where* the next earthquakes are likely to happen. The problem is, they don't have a good idea of *when*. That is why, despite incredible advances in seismology, the magnitude-7.6 quake that hit northwestern Pakistan on October 8, 2005, came without warning. Though comparable in strength to the 1906 San Francisco quake that killed 3,000 people, the tremor's multiple shocks and landslides in Pakistan destroyed thousands of buildings—**entire parts of towns were knocked off cliffs**—and took close to 90,000 lives, possibly more. When will the next one come? Who's to say?

# You know what you can do to stay safe from meteorites? Nothing.

In 1954, Ann Hodges was sleeping in her Sylacauga, Alabama, home when she was woken by an extraterrestrial. An 8.5-pound section of a 4.5-billion-year-old meteorite smashed into Hodges' home and hit its inhabitant, leaving a gruesome-looking bruise on her side. **She is the only known person to be injured by a meteorite,** despite between ten and fifty of them falling to Earth every day. (Oddly enough, Hodges' home was across the street from a movie theater called The Comet whose sign included a neon comet.) Hodges was featured on the cover of *Life* magazine and later used the cosmic rock as a doorstop. Although the impact didn't kill her, the stress of the incident and resulting media attention are suspected to have contributed to her early death at the age of fifty-two.

## Come to think of it, just stay inside.

Getting struck by lightning looks funny in a cartoon. In reality, it is a bit scarier. Nearly **thirty people die from lightning strikes every year** in the United States. However, they are not randomly distributed. Fatal lightning strikes are highly concentrated in specific states (Florida), months (July), times of the week (Saturday), location (outdoors, especially on the water), and gender (four out of five lightning deaths are male). Consider yourself warned, Floridian men who go boating on summer weekends.

# It's not the quicksand that gets you.

Any fan of classic cartoons knows that getting stuck in quicksand is a one-way ticket to a slow death. But in the real world (where road runners don't outsmart coyotes with ingenious traps), **quicksand alone rarely does anybody in.** Usually, it has help. In 2012, for example, thirty-three-year-old Nicola Raybone was watching the sunset from a beach in Antigua when she became stuck in quicksand. The poor woman died not from the quicksand but from drowning once the tide came in.

### SURVIVAL TIP

If you find yourself stuck in quicksand with a tide fast approaching, don't panic. Just wiggle one leg in small circles, slowly inching it up until it's free. Then kneel on your free leg, distributing weight evenly across your shin (so it doesn't get sucked in again), and start wiggling the stuck leg until you're out. Then you get to spend the rest of your life telling the "This is how I survived quicksand" story.

# Keep that epinephrine handy.

More people than ever have food allergies, including an estimated 33 million Americans, and experts aren't sure why. These allergies usually cause nothing more dangerous than dermatitis or hives. But some bodies respond to allergen exposure by going into anaphylactic shock, which can lead to death. While **having your throat close up after ingesting shellfish is a terrifying way to go,** it is also fairly uncommon. Food-induced anaphylaxis results in between 150 and 200 deaths per year. That may sound like a lot, but one academic study offered this reassuring comparison: you're more likely to be murdered than die from a food allergy.

## You will be conscious all the way down.

Some stories are told because they provide comfort, even about death. One frequently repeated trope has been the idea that a person falling from a great height is likely to pass out or die before hitting the ground. "I won't feel it when it happens" is a nice thought. But it is very difficult to field test, given the subjects' low survival rate, and almost certainly untrue. There is some possibility that a plummeting person could pass out from stress. But, for the most part, **a person falling to their death will be awake** long enough that their last thought will be, "Ouch." That's why it's best not to test gravity.

> *"The ocean is an object of no small terror."*
> —EDMUND BURKE

## Stay with the boat.

Over two million people visit the Great Barrier Reef off the northeast coast of Australia every year. Many dive underwater to see the reef up close. Nearly all survive the visit. In 1988, a tour boat 40 miles offshore loaded up its passengers and returned them to the mainland. Unfortunately, **they had forgotten two divers**: Americans Eileen and Tom Lonergan. Despite a large-scale search, the couple was sadly never found and, decades later, are presumed dead. Some of their gear washed up later, including a diving slate with the message, "We have been abandoned . . . Help!!!"

## Impatience can be deadly.

The tuberous root cassava originated in South America, but it is now one of the world's most popular starchy foods. A tentpole of West African cuisine, it can be fried, eaten as a cereal, or even used as flour. One handy tip: When preparing cassava, make sure you cook it really, really well. That's because raw sweet cassava **contains low levels of cyanide,** which is not something that adds to the enjoyment of a meal.

# Always bring your mittens.

The winter of 1887 to 1888 was punishing, even for cold-hardened Minnesotans. But things changed on January 12: the sky cleared, and the temperature soared high enough to melt some of the ice covering the state in its cruel grip. Farmers went out and did chores, and children left for school without their usual winter garb. That afternoon, **without warning, a thunderous blizzard covered the state,** blackening the sky, crashing the temperature, and filling the air with scathing ice pellets. Hundreds died in the heartbreakingly named "Children's Blizzard," which hit just as the kids were walking home from school.

## A fan can only do so much.

Fun fact for anyone visiting Europe in the summer: Many places there do not have air conditioning. It's just not a thing. This became particularly relevant in the summer of 2003, when the continent was hit by one of its worst-ever heat waves. The blistering temperatures **melted Alpine glaciers, set forests on fire, and caused droughts** that (because of nuclear power plants' need for water) reduced power when people needed it most. Tens of thousands died, including some who drowned when trying to cool themselves off by swimming.

# It's not that kind of hot spring.

Think a place like Yellowstone National Park is safe for visitors? "Ridiculous," wrote park historian Lee H. Whittlesey in his book *Death in Yellowstone*. "As if wilderness can be totally safe and still be wilderness." Just one part of Whittlesey's evidence? A number of fatal water burns. John Mark Williams, for example, was walking through a snowstorm in 1988 when he accidentally plunged into a hot spring. The 187-degree water **scalded him so horrifically his skin soon began peeling off** and he died later that night while being held by his terrified friends. He's one of more than twenty people killed by Yellowstone's 10,000 geysers, mud pots, steam vents, and hot springs, which is a good thing to remember the next time you decide to go off-trail.

# Water isn't antimicrobial.

Back in "the good old days," a person who got thirsty could generally find a drink of water at a well or public spigot. They just had to use a common cup or dipper, which was cleaned approximately never. Scientists realized this was a bad idea because of all the **diseases that spread via shared drinking vessels, like cholera and typhoid.** In 1907, that led Lawrence Luellen to invent the the Dixie Cup we know and have in our bathrooms today. It was a great step forward (for human health, not so much for the environment), but it hasn't stopped teenagers from sharing drinks and spreading deadly meningitis. The contagious bacteria kills between 150 and 300 Americans every year.

# Tap water isn't as clean as you think it is, either.

People with sinus issues are often advised to treat symptoms naturally using a neti pot—a kind of teapot for pouring water through your sinuses (which is as awkward as it sounds). In 2011, two unrelated Louisianans died after using neti pots. It was discovered they used tap water infected with *Naegleria fowleri*. **This is a rare but gross and vicious amoeba that causes dangerous brain swelling,** which is why it's also called the "brain-eating amoeba." *Naegleria fowleri* kills over 97 percent of infected people in just a few days. Had the victims imbibed the infected water, the amoeba would have been killed by their stomach acid. But introducing the water to their nostrils gave the amoeba a direct route to their brains.

# The world is only getting smaller.

If you lived in Europe during the "Black Death," the catchy name given to the bubonic plague that swept over the continent starting in the mid-fourteenth century, your chances of survival were . . . not great. About **one third to one half of all Europeans died** after a short period of wracking fever, shooting pain, and unpleasant things coming out of most orifices. The most lethal factor in the spread of the disease? It wasn't the rat population. It was the close proximity of people in densely populated cities and boats. So that bodes well for us today.

# The view from the top is really great, if you make it.

At just over 29,000 feet above sea level, Mount Everest is the highest mountain on Earth. For that reason, people really want to climb to the top of it. Everest is a forbidding peak in a very remote Himalayan mountain range lashed by severe storms, though, so occasionally, those climbers don't make it back. **About 1 percent of those who try to "summit" Everest die in the attempt.** Some of the hundreds of corpses are still up there, being stepped over by new climbers who are either tacky or dedicated, depending on your point of view.

# No, you won't fit.

How many people lie awake, worried about dying in a cave? More should. But twenty-six-year-old John Edward Jones was excited to crawl into the tight tunnels of Utah's Nutty Putty Cave in November 2009. He would never come out again. The medical student became stuck after entering an especially cramped section he mistook for another famously tight though navigable area known as the Birth Canal. **Rescue attempts only caused Jones more injuries.** After twenty-seven hours, the stress on his body became too much, and he died of cardiac arrest. Because Jones' body couldn't be recovered, the cave was sealed with concrete to become his tomb.

# Don't say, "It's only dust."

Images of the Dust Bowl during the Great Depression may look ominous, but not many would view them as scary. This indifferent attitude toward dust storms doesn't comport with reality, given that over **200 Americans died from what one study called "windblown dust events"** between 2007 and 2017. One of the places you are most likely to be murdered by a cloud of dust is the so-called "Deadliest 10 Miles" stretch of I-10 in Arizona between Phoenix and Tucson. The state has even implemented a "dust-storm warning system" in recent years. Snow and rain still outrank dust in terms of deadly weather events, but these giant walls of dirt and debris are not to be taken lightly.

# Small boat, big ocean, no problem?

The Clipper Round the World yacht race is the kind of thing that appeals to people who love the ocean and adventure but don't know a whole lot about racing yachts . . . or sailing, really. Featuring boats crewed by amateurs but with two pros on board, the biannual race takes up to eleven months to circumnavigate the Earth. Unsurprisingly, the combination of inexperience and wild ocean conditions sometimes leads to tragedy. In the 2015 race, **two people suffered fatal injuries on the same yacht:** Andrew Ashman was hit by the boom and, six months later, Sarah Young was swept overboard. After their deaths, applications for the race *increased*.

# Death by volcano is worse than you think.

It's easy to surmise that falling into a volcano will shorten your lifespan. But the manner of death is probably worse than you imagined. You do not, in fact, hit molten lava and die instantly. Instead, research suggests a person dropping into a pool of lava is **more likely to hit the semi-solid lava surface** and stay there for a time while slowly burning to death. If you ever find yourself wondering, the answer to "How close should I get to the rim of that active volcano?" is always, "Not close at all. Go the other way."

# At least death by ash is quick.

Tourists today idly wander the ruins of Italy's Pompeii and Herculaneum, towns frozen in time after being destroyed by the eruption of Mount Vesuvius. The ruins look quaint; what happened to them was anything but. When the volcano blew, it sent a terrifying swath of smoky ash through the towns. The ash suffocated some victims. But others died from the scorching heat wave (up to 900°F) that slashed across the region, **boiling people's blood and, in some cases, exploding their skulls.** So, if you have a choice between living near a volcano and not living near a volcano . . .

# Just enjoy your drink on shore.

Northern Georgia's Lake Lanier was created as an artificial reservoir in 1956 to generate water for Atlanta and hydroelectric power. The 58-square-mile lake became a popular recreation spot, with over 10 million visitors annually. It also became **the nation's most dangerous lake.** Roughly 700 people have died there since its creation. That death toll is shocking, but the reasons for it are not: most Lake Lanier visitors are recreational boaters, and a high percentage of them are A) some degree of intoxicated, and B) not wearing life jackets.

# Rivers giveth, and they certainly taketh away.

China's 3,900-mile-long Yangtze River had successfully nurtured early civilizations and watered the fertile floodplains of Central China without human intervention. Then farmers cut down its trees and built levees to direct flow, making it harder to manage runoff. That would have devastating consequences during 1931's extraordinarily wet summer. **In one month, the area got as much rain as it normally did in eighteen months, flooding an expanse the size of South Carolina.** Around 3.7 million people died (mostly from starvation and disease), making it the worst flood in recorded history and the century's most devastating natural disaster.

## Just because you can doesn't mean you should.

Even though Mont Blanc, the tallest mountain in the Alps at close to 16,000 feet, is not the hardest peak to summit in the world, it appears to be the most dangerous. Every summer, roughly 20,000 people try to climb it. Of those, **about 100 do not survive.** Some believe the fatality rate is so high because the relative simplicity of the climb leads to more inexperienced people trying it. (The gondolas that drop hikers off at 9,000 feet might also contribute to that misleading sense of ease.)

## You could just tell people you did it.

Back in 1865, a report on the Half Dome—a massive rock formation looming about 5,000 feet over Yosemite National Park—said it "never has been, and never will be, trodden by human foot." Maybe that writer meant "never should be." By 2010, so many people were trying to climb up to its summit that the National Park Service started requiring permits. They originally limited them to 300 a day but changed to a lottery system after selling out in an hour. The climbers seem undeterred by the **more than sixty deaths that have occurred on the Half Dome** and the trail leading to it from things like falls, heart attacks, and lightning strikes.

## The healing power of plants is nothing compared to their deadliness.

Jane Percy, the Duchess of Northumberland, spent years upscaling the centuries-old 14-acre Alnwick Garden she inherited, and she decided she wanted something different. Things that can kill seemed like a good attraction. That's how the infamous Poison Garden was created. Today, visitors can **venture past the looming black gates with the skull and crossbones** and look at (but not touch!) dozens of fatal plants, such as hemlock and deadly nightshade. The garden is always guarded, and many exhibits are locked up because some of the plants are deadly even to the touch, and people can be, well . . . you know. Each year, dozens faint just from smelling the plants they were warned not to smell.

## Next time, don't stop to smell the roses.

Despite being built back in 1350 in the Netherlands, which saw its share of battles over the years, Geldrop Castle has never had much violence attached to it. That changed in August 2022, when the local Highland Games (Scottish heritage celebrations held around the world) were being held at the castle. Geldrop also features gardens that attract tourists, one of whom happened to be wandering the grounds when a Highland gamer in the hammer-throw event **launched his 22-pound metal hammer over a hedge.** A witness said the victim never saw the hammer coming, which was probably for the best.

# You never know when the ground will give way.

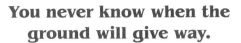

Sinkholes are an unusual though less-rare-than-is-comforting phenomenon in which the ground under the surface can't support its weight anymore. They are often created by water wearing away softer rocks. Sinkholes happen in the strangest places, like the villa outside Tel Aviv, Israel, where one developed underneath a swimming pool and **sucked a swimmer dozens of feet below ground to his death.** The fact that the pool's owners never went through the permitting process didn't help. But some areas, including Israel and states like Pennsylvania and Florida, are just prone to these unpredictable collapses.

## SURVIVAL TIP

Sinkholes are notoriously hard to spot, but there are a few warning signs. In a house, look for doors that no longer latch, cracks in walls and over doorways, and new water leaks. When outside, a circular dip in the earth; an oddly deep, round puddle; and cracking pavement can all be red flags and reasons to give a place a wide berth.

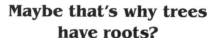

*"Poor decisions and bad luck are contingencies
of most horror films."*
—WESLEY MORRIS

## Maybe that's why trees
## have roots?

Oudenaarde is a medieval market town in Belgium's Flemish region, featuring gorgeous buildings from the Middle Ages. It's also home to an annual holiday market, which in 2023 included a beautiful Christmas tree, blazing with lights, that towered 65 feet high. But when a storm blew through the Low Countries in late December, **the five-ton tree fell, killing a sixty-three-year-old woman** and injuring two others. The tree was certainly spectacular, but "large enough to crush a person" seems to fall into the "too large" category.

## That must have been
## some chicken.

A string of unexpected tragedies followed a seemingly minor incident in the southern Egyptian village of Nazlat Imara in August 1995. When a chicken fell into a 60-foot-deep well, an eighteen-year-old farmer went after it. **He was sucked in by an undercurrent and drowned.** Then his sister tried to rescue him, and she also drowned. Then his brother. Then his other brother. Then two more farmers. All of them drowned, but the chicken made it out alive.

# Look up.

When hiking, careful people have a lot to look out for: snakes, chasms, and bear tracks, to name a few. The same goes for driving: You have to look out for pedestrians, animals, and, especially, other drivers. With their eyes so firmly fixed on their immediate surroundings, people don't often think to glance upward. According to one study, around **400 have died between 1955 and 2007 from "wind-related tree failures"** (translation: trees falling over). Roughly half of those cases involved cars—either they drove into a fallen tree, or a tree toppled onto their car. Whether a sunroof would be helpful or dangerous in these situations is up for debate.

# Natural materials are not always better.

History is filled with stories of fires that burned all or large parts of cities. Many of these metropolises had something in common: they were made mostly of wood. The "Great Fires" of 1871 that scorched America's Upper Midwest (Chicago, Michigan, Wisconsin) were fueled in part by wood infrastructure. The 1945 U.S. bombing raid on Tokyo created a napalm-fueled firestorm that **wiped out 16 square miles of the city's mostly wood-and-paper buildings and killed more than 80,000 people.** Builders could have predicted the latter disaster after a similar reliance on wood in Tokyo made possible the fires following the 1923 earthquake that killed at least 120,000. But it takes us humans a while to learn from mistakes.

# Let's *not* go fly a kite.

One day in early 2022, thirteen-year-old Anirudh Machad was out flying a kite in the Sahar neighborhood of Mumbai, India. This is not uncommon in the city, where kite flying is so popular that police started cracking down on it in some areas. But most kite-flying sessions don't end the way Machad's did. Many of Mumbai's coconut trees were damaged and falling over, partially due to the cyclones that wracked the city. As Machad concentrated on his kite, **a coconut palm snapped and fell on the poor boy,** killing him instantly.

# We're going to need a bigger boat.

Fossil fuels would be awesome if their use didn't cause ice at the poles to melt, which, in turn, causes sea levels to rise. In the future, entire countries could be impacted. Scientists believe the Maldives—the nation with the world's lowest elevation and half a million people scattered across an Indian Ocean archipelago— will be **80 percent uninhabitable by the year 2050** and entirely swallowed up by the ocean before 2100. People may have to abandon it even earlier, because salt water is polluting the islands' water supply. (It may be a good time to invest in a boat and some solar panels.)

# A car is basically an oven on wheels.

Incredibly, many people still don't realize how dangerous it is to leave a child or animal in a car. **About thirty-eight children younger than fifteen years old die annually from heatstroke induced by sitting in a hot car**—sometimes in as little as ten minutes. In about half of these cases, the adult did not intentionally leave the child behind but forgot they were there. When it comes to pets, leaving them is usually intentional, and the number is in the hundreds. The CDC warns that the inside of a car can hit 109°F in just 20 minutes on a breezy 80°F day. And no, cracking a window does not help. Save that Target run for a day when you're alone.

# Stubble might be safer.

Michael F. Farley was an immigrant success story, until he wasn't. Born in Ireland, Farley came to America as a teenager in 1881, ran a saloon, and was elected to Congress. He was described by a newspaper as "a power" in New York's infamous Tammany Hall political machine. All that came to an end in 1921. **Farley checked into Bellevue Hospital with a swollen neck after cutting himself shaving and died just hours later.** It turned out that the brush he used for shaving cream lather was infected with anthrax, which hitched a ride on its imported animal hair. Not the legacy most powerful politicos want to leave.

# Rust gets a bad rap.

Back in the day, if you got a minor cut, there was a small chance of your dying anyway. That is because of the bacterium *Clostridium tetani*. Its omnipresent spores are very eager to get inside a wound so they can cause tetanus. They hitch a ride on things like nails, rusty or not. Until vaccines became common in the 1940s, this could cause **lockjaw, the symptoms of which are partially self-explanatory but also include death.** Thanks to the availability of vaccines, tetanus fatalities continue to plummet, from over a quarter-million in 1990 to under 35,000 in 2019. But again, that's still greater than zero, so look out for those rusty nails.

## SURVIVAL TIP

Vaccines are the first line of defense. But if you do step on a nail, the next thing you should do is wash your hands so you don't make things worse. (Bacteria's the problem, remember?) Then apply pressure to stop the bleeding, rinse the wound with clean water for five to ten minutes, and apply an ointment and a bandage. And, obviously, if anything starts oozing, go to a doctor.

"Some people
are so afraid
to die that they
never begin
to live."

—HENRY VAN DYKE

## Chapter 6

# HISTORIC
# ENDINGS

# Last call . . . really.

An old English folk ditty praises the "mellow" man who "drinks strong ale" and "dies a jolly good fellow." There is no way of knowing how mellow the residents of London's St Giles neighborhood were when **a massive barrel of porter at their local brewery burst open** on October 17, 1814. What is known is that hundreds of thousands of gallons of beer flooded the streets. Eight residents died in the sudsy tide, and many more lost their homes. Rumors that some in the poverty-stricken area were lapping up puddles of beer seem less evidence of bad decision-making than of the stubborn persistence of British classism.

## Every now and then, infrastructure simply requires a human sacrifice.

Frustrated by how the rushing water and soft riverbed damaged construction of Japan's Ohashi Bridge in the seventeenth century, workers resorted to a tried-and-true solution: human sacrifice. Legend has it that several **old buildings and bridges throughout the country have the bodies of some unfortunate victims of hitobashira moldering somewhere inside to steady the structures.** Ohashi's workers decided the first man to cross the still-unfinished bridge wearing *hakama* trousers would be the lucky winner. An ill-fated local named Gensuke, who happened to be wearing the fatal pants, was duly grabbed and buried in the riverbed under the bridge's middle stretch, strengthening it for centuries. (And likely reducing the demand for *hakama* pants.)

## Hell hath no fury like
## a mother scorned.

One of the many concubine consorts for China's Emperor Xuanwu, Hu Guozhen did what women in her position rarely did: she prayed for a son. Back then, the custom was to kill the mother of a crown prince. But Hu wanted to ensure the line of succession. And she did, with her son Yuan Xu, who would become Emperor Xiaoming in 515 BCE. Hu was spared, but she wasn't as merciful herself. **Not only did she arbitrarily execute many subjects as Empress Dowager, she eventually poisoned Xiaoming.** (To be fair, the teenage emperor had her boyfriend killed, and even mothers have their limits.) Hu was drowned in the Yellow River as punishment.

## Stay away if the boss
## is feeling sick.

During Egypt's First Dynasty, the country's rulers had a peculiar habit. Believing a comfortable afterlife depended on having their servants with them, they wanted to be buried with as many as possible. **Enter: retainer sacrifice—killing servants and burying them with their masters.** This is why the tombs of kings from that period often contain the remains of dozens, if not hundreds, of people. While the estimated ages of the dead suggest untimely ends, respectful burials and a lack of violent injuries suggest they were at least somewhat merciful. Either way, hearing the king had passed had to make for an uncomfortable moment in the court.

The Little Book of Horrors

# Some gurus don't know
# when to die.

Nicholas II and Alexandra, the doomed final couple of Russia's Romanov Dynasty, never understood why everybody hated their beloved mystic Rasputin. By 1917, rumors of "the mad monk" Rasputin's drunkenness, lechery, and supposedly hypnotic power over the tsar and tsarina were so widespread that an assassination plot was hatched. It almost didn't work. **Cyanide-laced cakes? Nope. Cyanide wine? That didn't do it.** So they shot him, only for Rasputin to get up and try to stumble out of the St. Petersburg palace where his inept assassins were gathered. He was then shot *again*, beaten, and, for good measure, tied up and hurled into the ice-cold Neva River where he finally died. Probably.

# A safety is no replacement
# for common sense.

In 1871, famous American politician and lawyer Clement Vallandigham was in Ohio defending one Thomas McGehan, who was charged with murdering a man he had supposedly been feuding with. Vallandigham planned a courtroom spectacle by demonstrating that the shooting couldn't have happened the way the witnesses claimed it did. Unfortunately, when practicing the big move in his hotel room, **Vallandigham picked up the wrong pistol.** His final words: "I have foolishly shot myself." Illustrating the thin line between comedy and tragedy, McGehan was acquitted but ended up shot dead himself not long later.

# Laughter is not always the best medicine.

Known as the "Second Founder of Stoicism," Chrysippus of Soli worked hard to make up for not starting this famously unfunny school of philosophy before its founder, Zeno of Citium. Chrysippus published hundreds of books and is revered today by classical scholars. But even philosophers let loose every now and again. While smashed on wine at a party in 206 BCE, **Chrysippus saw a donkey eating a fig and broke out laughing.** And he kept laughing. And laughing. And then he died, supposedly after shouting (while still laughing), "Give the donkey a drink of pure wine to wash down the figs!" (Maybe you had to be there?)

# Don't blame the mastermind, blame the horses.

In 1258, the Mongol ruler Hulagu was conquering everything he could point his mounted armies at. Eventually, his eyes turned to the Abbasid caliphate in modern-day Iraq. After capturing their capital, Baghdad, Hulagu decided to execute the Abbasid caliph (spiritual leader). Because caliphs were considered sacred, he was worried this would lead to calamity. **Hulagu ordered the caliph to be rolled up in a rug and stomped to death by horses,** which he figured kept his hands clean. There is no record of what fate befell those murdering horses.

# Don't cross a royal.

The best advice to anybody considering expressing their displeasure against the English crown in the Middle Ages would have been: *don't*. Until clarified by the Treason Act of 1351, *treason* was defined as essentially anything the royal court thought it was. The punishment for this vague crime was drawing and quartering. What's that? Well, it was also nebulous, but it could include hanging until only *mostly* dead, followed by live disemboweling, beheading, and occasionally **tying each of the prisoner's limbs to horses, which were then spurred to race off in opposite directions.** That seems like overkill, but then, "medieval" never meant "nice" or "forgiving."

## Public decency is little consolation when being burned alive.

Whereas men convicted of treason in ye olde England were drawn and quartered, female traitors had a different end waiting for them: being burned at the stake. Why the gender separation, you ask? It was apparently for their own good. Renowned legal expert William Blackstone wrote in the 1760s that **dying in slow, excruciating pain was better for women because at least they stayed fully clothed.** He argued that "the decency due to the sex forbids the exposing and publicly mangling their bodies." Despite that small mercy, Blackstone did point out that being burnt alive feels "as terrible" as more male-centric executions.

# Just wash your hands. Please.

Many people don't remember that "Typhoid Mary" was an actual person. Irish-born Mary Mallon emigrated to America in the 1880s and became a cook. Between 1900 and 1907, twenty-two people caught typhoid in houses where Mary worked. Even after Mary discovered she was a "healthy carrier" of the deadly disease, she refused to stop handling food. **She was finally forced into quarantine after infecting hundreds of people and killing at least three.** And that's why you don't go to work sick.

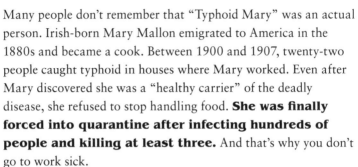

### SURVIVAL TIP

As we learned from Mary, asymptomatic transmission is a thing. Hand sanitizer is helpful, but there are several germs it doesn't kill—including norovirus, the highly contagious stomach bug no one wants but hundreds of people catch every year on crowded and invariably filthy cruise ships. And it can live on practically any surface. So washing your hands with soap and water for the recommended 20 seconds really is a life (and stomach) saver.

# Fling out your dead.

Things were bad enough for residents of the Crimean city of Kaffa in 1343. That year, the so-called "Golden Horde," a massive Mongol army decimating everything in its path, laid siege to the city. Then Mongol forces started dropping like flies—flies with the bubonic plague. But before Kaffa's starving residents could celebrate, the Mongol khan Jani Beg decided to take one last shot at his enemies. **The Mongols loaded their diseased dead onto catapults and began hurling them over Kaffa's walls** like extremely gross medieval biological weapons. In an effort to escape disease, residents boarded ships to Italy. And the rest was plague history.

## Slow down . . . maybe chew your food.

Fat Tuesday is the feast day for Christians looking to pack in a few extra calories before the privation of Lent. While the point of the day is excess, some take it too far. Like Sweden's King Adolf Frederick. A well-found gourmand, Adolf did not disappoint on Fat Tuesday in 1771. That year, **the king's spread included piles of lobster, caviar, and smoked herring along with champagne.** But he overdid it with dessert. The king loved semla (Swedish pastry buns crammed with almond paste and whipped cream) so much that he gobbled up fourteen of them. He didn't live to see Wednesday. Whether it was poison or a heart attack from overindulgence, no one can say.

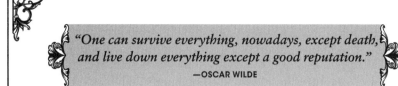

## Curiosity killed the world-renowned scientist.

In 1626, famed scholar and scientist Sir Francis Bacon was in London having a chat with a friend about preserving food, as one does. Inspired by an idea, Bacon bought a (dead) chicken and packed it with ice, thinking (correctly) this was a good way to safely store meat. **While Bacon's science was solid, his appreciation of the elements was less so.** Gathering that ice in the cold caused him to catch a cold that turned into pneumonia, which killed him soon after. However, all reports indicate the chicken still tasted delicious.

## John Wayne's worst role might have killed him.

Even John Wayne fans had a hard time taking him seriously as Mongol warlord Genghis Khan in the 1956 turkey *The Conqueror*. The movie featured epic battle scenes, Wayne's horrible mustache, and stunning desert locations shot in a part of Nevada unfortunately still **covered in radioactive fallout from the atomic bombs previously tested nearby.** Nearly half the cast and crew were eventually diagnosed with cancer, and dozens (including the Duke himself) succumbed to it. And on top of it all, the movie was terrible.

# They really did dance 'til they dropped.

Long before the people of Strasbourg, Alsace (modern-day France), ever heard the terms "disco" or "Eurotrash," they discovered that dancing came with a price. In the summer of 1518, a Strasbourg woman named Frau Troffea started dancing alone in the street outside her home. Her manic stylings went on for days and gathered imitators. **Soon, hundreds of so-called "choreomaniacs" were flailing about in fits of ecstasy, some until they died of exhaustion.** Fears of choreomania led authorities to temporarily ban all music and dancing. Call it *Footloose: Holy Roman Empire Edition*.

# One person's drunken death is another's liability issue.

Church bells were important to many communities throughout history. Besides signaling worship times, they announced when people should gather, if danger was afoot, or that a celebration was called for. One night in November 1592, residents of Cobham, England, were having a jolly old (inebriated) time at one such occasion when bell-ringer John Robinson stood up on a bench to grab the bell's rope. **Somehow, the rope looped around the bench and yanked it into the air.** Robinson was pitched off, cracked his head, and died soon after. In other words, his death was exactly the kind of thing personal injury lawyers were invented for.

# It wasn't "the noble experiment" they envisioned.

Prohibition, America's experiment with enforced sobriety from 1920 to 1933, is remembered largely for how much it did not work. Certain people (flappers, gangsters, proto-NASCAR rum runners) had quite a lot of fun flouting the law. And it turns out that giving people no alternative to homemade alcohol can be a tad risky. **Roughly 1,000 people died annually from drinking bad hooch during the Prohibition era.** (Something to remember the next time weird Uncle Beau offers a sample of his garage moonshine.)

# You never know who's holding a grudge.

John Kendrick became a wealthy hero seizing British ships during the American Revolution. After the war, he burnished his résumé by exploring and opening trade across the Pacific. He docked in Honolulu in 1794, just in time to help Hawaiian King Kamehameha fight off a rival with his crew and that of a British ship. The next day, Kendrick and the British captain celebrated victory by firing off multi-cannon salutes. The British, however, **fired a live round of grapeshot, killing Kendrick and several of his officers.** They said it was a mistake, but there may have been some residual British grumpiness about the Revolution.

# Being licensed to practice medicine should really be the bare minimum.

In the early twentieth century, the state of Washington licensed people as "fasting specialists." One was "Doctor" Linda Hazzard (she had no medical training), who thought occasional semi-starvation was one way to good health. At least a dozen patients died from her alternative cures, which included **sustained fasting, aggressive massages, and many enemas.** But that might have been the goal. Hazzard also had a habit of seizing her patients' money and property—clothes, jewels, even land. Still, she practiced what she preached, dying in 1938 after trying her very own fasting cure.

# Don't worry—it's just a balloon. Right?

When Reverend Archie Mitchell and his pregnant wife, Elsie, took five children from Archie's Sunday-school class for a morning picnic on May 5, 1945, peace seemed near. The Nazis had surrendered, and the Japanese Empire was on its last legs. And the couple were in Oregon, nowhere near the fray. **But when Archie went to grab lunch from the car, there was an explosion.** Elsie and the children had been killed by one of the Japanese bomb-carrying balloons designed to ride the jet stream across the ocean. They were the only Americans killed on the mainland by enemy action in World War II.

# The squeaky wheel
# gets greased.

Ottavio Bottecchia was one of the most popular figures in 1920s Italy. A champion bicyclist, he won the Tour de France in 1924 and 1925. He was also outspoken about the fascists taking over his country. **This is why some were suspicious when Bottecchia turned up bloodied, beaten, and dead in 1927.** One of the more ridiculous claims was that he died after a beating from a furious vineyard owner whose grapes Bottecchia had snaked. But a more likely explanation cropped up later, when an Italian immigrant on his deathbed in New York confessed that he had been hired by fascists to murder Bottecchia.

# He thought he could make it.

When Croxton, England, laborer Robert Bakar was trying to quickly get from the parish church to the rectory on Christmas Day 1521, he figured he could be forgiven for finding a shortcut. Unfortunately for him, that shortcut involved leaping over a pond using a "heggestake" (a kind of pole). **It snapped in half, sending Baker into the water, where he drowned.** Centuries later, athletes would repeat his feat over dry land for sport, with sometimes similarly disastrous results.

# Don't believe everything you read.

Nobody likes to be reminded of their own mortality, let alone have it printed for everybody (including yourself) to read about. In 1940, years after legal troubles and the collapse of his "back to Africa" movement drove him out of the United States, Black nationalist leader Marcus Garvey was living in retirement in London. One day, he picked up a copy of the *Chicago Defender* and saw his own name. **To his dismay, the paper not only included his premature obituary but described him as "broke, alone, and unpopular."** He soon proved the obituary right, dying of a stroke just two weeks later.

### SURVIVAL TIP

Stress kills. And so do strokes if you don't get to the doctor in time to treat them. Just remember to "be fast": balance problems, eyesight issues, face drooping, arm weakness, and speech difficulty mean it's time to call 9-1-1. And actually *be fast*—the sooner you get medical attention, the better your odds of survival.

# Add "no taxidermy"
# to the will.

Julia Pastrana was a Mexican woman who became famous in the nineteenth century—not for anything she did, but for the unfortunate thing her husband did. Pastrana suffered from generalized hypertrichosis, **a rare affliction that makes hair grow all over a person's face,** as well as gingival hyperplasia, a condition that gave her irregular teeth and gums. But she used it to her advantage, earning money by appearing in sideshows that also displayed her talents and intellect. After she died from childbirth in 1860, Pastrana's husband kept the gravy train rolling by taxidermizing her body and hauling it around the world.

## Dying in your sleep isn't
## always peaceful.

Almost everyone has had one nightmare that made them anxious about going to bed. That's why horror flicks like *A Nightmare on Elm Street*, in which a demonic figure named Freddy murders teenagers in their dreams, are so effective. While the movie's story was fictional, its inspiration was not. Director Wes Craven's imagination was spurred by **stories about Cambodian refugees in America who died in their sleep with no apparent causes.** The best explanation doctors had was that the horrors refugees experienced in the Khmer Rouge's savage civil war created buried trauma that literally frightened them to death later.

# When in doubt,
# keep it short.

When William Henry Harrison took the inaugural stage as the newly elected president on March 4, 1841, he had a lot of things to say. *A lot*. Harrison finished delivering his speech a record-breaking two hours later. Besides exhausting the audience with classical Roman allusions, the sixty-eight-year-old Harrison also exhausted himself by speaking so long outside on a chilly day without an overcoat or hat. **The president developed pneumonia and died a month later** despite various pre-modern medical interventions. (Somehow, using heated suction cups to "draw out" the sickness failed to work.)

# Blame it on the mailman. And be
# grateful for texting.

The Battle of New Orleans was one of the great American victories against the British in the War of 1812. In late December 1814, General Andrew Jackson organized a hasty defense of the city. When the British launched their assault on January 8, they were routed in just a couple hours, suffering more than 2,000 casualties compared to fewer than 100 on the American side. But **each of those deaths, wounds, and captures was gratuitous** because the war had been over since the Treaty of Ghent was signed on December 24. "If we had had the cable telegraph in those days, this blood would not have been spilt," wrote Mark Twain. "Better still, Jackson would probably never have been president."

# Seriously, don't tempt fate.

During the Civil War, John Sedgwick was one of the most competent officers in the Union Army, a force not known for having a surplus of such men. He was also lauded for his bravery. At the start of the Battle of Spotsylvania Court House in 1864, Sedgwick admonished his men, who were ducking for cover, by saying the enemy "couldn't hit an elephant at this distance." That was the moment **a Confederate sharpshooter put a bullet in his head.** Despite his ironic passing, Sedgwick's heroic reputation was enough to have a fort and multiple streets (in Chicago and the Bronx) named for him.

# Werewolf or serial killer: which is worse?

In 1589, a German man named Peter Stubbe (or sometimes Stumpp) was charged with being a werewolf. Though charges of witchcraft were more common, this sort of thing occasionally happened to people in pre-modern times. But charges of sorcerous lycanthropy aside (a magic belt and a pact with the devil were involved), **Stubbe may have been an actual serial killer and cannibal.** He confessed to having murdered and eaten fourteen children and two pregnant women, along with a number of cows. Suffice it to say that when he was flayed alive and beheaded, few mourned.

# Don't be so quick to prove yourself.

By 1918, World War I had been grinding on for four years with not much to show for it but some good poetry and millions of lives lost. On November 11, the American infantry was facing the Germans near Meuse, France. Both sides were still, waiting for the Armistice, when **Private Henry N. Gunther got up and charged the enemy.** Even they tried to wave him off, but he fired a shot and was cut down by a quick spurt of machine-gun fire at 10:58 a.m. Two minutes later, the Armistice went into effect, ending the war. This made Gunther the conflict's last and most confusing combat death. If nothing else, his action proves the military adage: "Never volunteer for anything."

## At least capital punishment has evolved. Kind of.

If there's one thing humans are good at, it's inventing new ways to kill other humans. That's how we got crucifixion. Although it's mainly associated with the Romans' execution of Jesus Christ, crucifixion was used several hundred years earlier. Persia's King Darius I crucified 3,000 Babylonians at once in 519 BCE. In this archaic form of capital punishment, a prisoner was tied or nailed to a crossbeam hoisted 10 or more feet up, then fixed to a vertical pole *after* being beaten and scourged with whips. **They were then left to die slowly from asphyxiation or blood loss.** Fortunately, the modern world is more humane, instead scorching the condemned with electricity or suffocating them with poison gas.

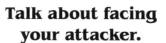

# Talk about facing
# your attacker.

Some death row prisoners are given a nice last feast, a tradition
that began in ancient Greece to avoid creating a hungry ghost.
Convicted murderer Susanna Margarethe Brandt enjoyed one of
the stranger versions of a last meal in Frankfurt, Germany, circa
1772. She had a choice of sausage, beef, roast veal, soup, and a
nice 1748 vintage wine, all shared with local officials and judges.
In nearby Bavaria around the same time period, a tradition
known as St. John's Blessing saw the condemned not only enjoy
a lavish final meal but also **share a final drink with their
executioner.** That likely made for awkward conversation
("So . . . what kind of sword are you going to use?").

# Even the Romans thought Celtic
# rituals were a bit much.

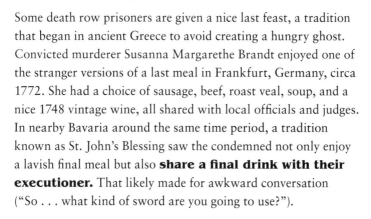

When the Romans conquered the British Isles, they decided the
Celts were savages and tried to exterminate them. Though tales
of Celtic barbarism were long considered Roman propaganda,
archaeological discoveries later revealed that there may have been
a grain of truth to the rumors. One preserved Iron Age nobleman
was found **stabbed and sawn in half, missing his
nipples, with rope threaded through holes in his
arms.** An Irish antiquities specialist told a newspaper that ritual
killings of Celtic kings "tend to be excessive," which feels like an
understatement.

# Bad horror-movie plot or actual historical horror?

If Julius Caesar can be believed, the Romans had even more reason to be frightened of the Celts than their treatment of kings. According to Caesar's *Commentaries of the Gallic War*, as well as accounts from other Roman writers, Celtic priests known as **Druids liked sacrificing men by sticking them inside giant wicker statues and setting them on fire.** They preferred to sacrifice criminals, but they would use any hapless passerby in a pinch. Anybody who has seen *The Wicker Man*— either the 1973 original or the 2006 remake with a yowling Nicolas Cage—can appreciate how effective a motivational tool this was for keeping people off the wrong side of Druids.

# It's a calling.

One of history's most famous executioners was William Marwood, a Lincolnshire, England, cobbler who decided in 1872, at the age of fifty-four, to change jobs. He saw the then-prevalent method of hanging as needlessly cruel. His method, the "long drop," **killed with a sudden breaking of the neck instead of slow strangulation.** Harwood killed 176 people this way, getting a £10 bonus for each one. He took the job seriously, soothingly whispering to the condemned, "I will not hurt you; it will soon be over." He also printed business cards that read, "William Marwood, Executioner," just in case he ran across anybody needing his services.

# Watch your wine intake in mixed company.

Those who ran afoul of powerful people in ancient Persia could be shown their mistakes in a very gruesome way. The "torture of the boats," or scaphism, was an ordeal in which two boats or logs were fitted together around the victim, with holes cut so their limbs and head stuck out. Then the victim's face was slathered in milk and honey, attracting flies. As the days passed, **the covered areas of the body were agonizingly consumed by maggots.** One victim—Mithridates I of Pontus, who contradicted King Artaxerxes of Persia—lasted seventeen days. The reason he chose to run his mouth? He had been drinking and, as the Greeks said, *in vino veritas*.

# Bad news for anyone who thought death was the end.

Many Catholics had negative feelings about Pope Formosus, who was once excommunicated, later became Pope, and then made enemies by engaging in political intrigue and king-making shenanigans. About nine months after Formosus's death in 896, authorities **dug up his corpse so they could put him on trial for many charges,** including perjury. After being found guilty in the so-called "Cadaver Synod," they condemned Formosus's memory and cut the fingers he had used for blessings off his body before tossing it into the Tiber River. (Seems like overkill.)

# He was going to live forever, even if it killed him.

Qin Shi Huang was the first emperor to unify China after the chaotic Warring States period. But this wasn't enough for the overachiever; he wanted to live forever. He became obsessed, seeking out increasingly arcane elixirs that promised to substantiate his chosen name: "The Immortal." But no one who chooses their own nickname succeeds. Eventually, as the story goes, **the emperor imbibed a concoction that promised eternal life but contained mercury,** which tends to do the opposite. He died of mercury poisoning in 210 BCE at the age of forty-nine.

# General rule: Fans should keep their clothes to themselves.

Legendary Athenian lawmaker Draco (of the seventh century BCE) didn't care about adulation. He created a system of legal punishments so harsh that his name became a byword for overly punitive—*draconian.* Despite the severe criminal penalties, the people loved him. **In fact, their adulation was so overwhelming that it killed him.** At his last public event, Draco was showered with so many hats and clothes (which was apparently how Athenians showed appreciation) that he suffocated.

# Other than that,
# how was the show?

Anybody attending a show at a grand Chicago theater today takes some things for granted: exit doors opening outward instead of inward, "panic bars" for emergency exits, and fireproofed scenery. This is largely due to the devastating tragedy of December 30, 1903. That day, a packed house of 1,700 at the brand-new Iroquois Theater panicked when a stage light set the drapery alight. **Curtains obscured the exits, there were more patrons than seats, and locked gates made the balconies inescapable.** The theater, which had been billed as "absolutely fireproof" had violated every possible safety regulation. Over 600 people died in less than half an hour. Soon after, new building ordinances swept through the city like the fire that inspired them.

## SURVIVAL TIP

The story of Qin Shi Huang accidentally poisoning himself sounds far-fetched, but plenty of people today take unregulated supplements without thinking twice about it. Unnecessary dietary supplements alone send more than 23,000 people to the emergency room each year. Before you take anything—even if it's "natural"—talk to your doctor and get a full workup. And maybe, instead of gulping down vitamin C pills, just eat an orange.

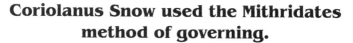

# Coriolanus Snow used the Mithridates method of governing.

Mithridates VI of Pontus (aka Mithridates the Great), an emperor who ruled in northern Anatolia from 120 to 63 BCE, is remembered for two things: trying to fight off the vastly superior Roman Empire and slowly poisoning himself. Known as the "Poisoner King," he was led by pharmacological fascinations to **not only poison his enemies but also inoculate himself with tiny doses of poison** in case anyone tried to return the favor. The self-administered antidotes worked a little too well, foiling his plan to commit suicide after being defeated by the Romans. When his poison failed, and assumedly in great pain, Mithridates had his bodyguard administer a fatal blow via sword.

# Consider the odds before plotting your escape.

According to the Alcatraz hype, the maximum-security federal penitentiary, which sat on an island surrounded by the San Francisco Bay's nasty currents, was escape-proof. That didn't stop inmates from trying. **Of thirty-six escapees, twenty-three were caught, seven were shot and killed, and three or more drowned.** The most dramatic attempt was in 1946, when inmates seized weapons and took officers hostage, setting off a two-day gun battle that ended when the Marines stormed in with firebombs. Three of the six inmates were killed in the fighting, and two others were executed, which works out to a not-great 17 percent survival rate. And the one who survived was sentenced to ninety-nine more years in prison.

## Cheaters never prosper.

In the late ninth century, the Orkney and Shetland islands were ruled by the Viking warlord Sigurd Eysteinsson. He gained the nickname "Sigurd the Mighty" after conquering the Scottish Highlands. Sigurd challenged one Scottish chieftain—Máel Bigte the Bucktoothed—to a battle where each agreed to bring forty men. Sigurd cheated and brought eighty, earning an easy, if dishonest, victory. But irony had the upper hand. After Sigurd decapitated Máel and latched the head to his saddle, **a protruding bucktooth opened a wound in Sigurd's leg.** This being the ninth century, the scratch led to infection led to sepsis led to the end of Sigurd the Cheater.

## Just put out the fire.

On April 16, 1947, the SS *Grandcamp* and SS *High Flyer* docked in the port of Texas City (near Galveston, Texas), packing a total of over 3,000 tons of ammonium nitrate fertilizer. That morning, a fire broke out in the *Grandcamp* cargo hold, and the crew made a fatal mistake, considering their cargo. To avoid getting the fertilizer wet, they tried to snuff out the flames by forcing steam into the cargo hold—which had the opposite effect. **The resulting detonation wiped out the dock area, sent up a mushroom cloud, and even took out two planes overhead.** Worse still, fiery shrapnel ignited the *High Flyer*, which also exploded. At least 500 people died in what has been deemed America's worst-ever industrial accident.

# Definitely don't walk
## *toward* the fire.

During World War I, Nova Scotia's Halifax Harbor bustled with shipping. Since it was wartime, that meant munitions. On December 6, 1917, the Norwegian refugee relief ship SS *Imo* was leaving the port when it collided with the SS *Mont-Blanc*, a French freighter packed with thousands of tons of munitions. The *Mont-Blanc* caught fire, and its crew wisely abandoned ship. It then drifted into the pier, where crowds unwisely gathered to watch the blaze. Then **the ship exploded with the force of almost 3,000 tons of TNT,** wiping out most of the port and killing nearly 2,000 people instantly.

# We have met the enemy,
# and they are us.

Any general worried about their battlefield record just needs to read about the Battle of Karánsebes in 1788 to feel better. This accidental intramural skirmish in the Austro-Turkish War was started when **some Austrian cavalrymen had too much schnapps.** They got into an argument with some of their own infantry, who simply wanted to join the revelry, and that led to a fist fight, mass confusion, and random gunfire. This sparked panic in the army's camp, leading to artillery fusillades and a full-on Austrian-on-Austrian gunfight. When the Turks showed up a couple days later, the Austrians were already gone, having left 10,000 casualties behind.

# No one likes a flip-flopper.

George Plantagenet, Duke of Clarence, was one of those conspiratorial royals who made the Wars of the Roses so fascinating (and so hard to follow). Raised in the House of York, Clarence backed his brother Edward when he became King Edward IV. But then Clarence changed his mind and threw his support behind the deposed Henry VI. Clarence eventually flopped back to the Yorkists, **but not in time to avoid a treason charge.** He was drowned in a wine cask at the Tower of London in 1478. Clarence's death is waggishly foreshadowed in Shakespeare's *Richard III*, when his character is told, "You shall have wine enough, my lord."

# A little death, literally and figuratively.

Peter Anthony Motteux (1663–1718) would have wanted to be remembered more for his life than his death. Born in Rouen, he resettled in England because of anti-Huguenot prejudice. He became a renowned playwright, translator, disputatious literary wit, and dealer of Asian artifacts. Unfortunately for Motteux, the circumstances of his passing overshadowed all of that. This Renaissance man was the **first-known fatal case of autoerotic asphyxia** (strangulation for erotic pleasure). Adding to the distinction, he was assisted by a prostitute, and it was his fifty-fifth birthday. His epitaph reads in part, "Died the day he was born / By squeezing his collar too tightly."

> *"A common mistake that people make when trying to design something completely foolproof is to underestimate the ingenuity of complete fools."*
> **—DOUGLAS ADAMS**

## Design flaw or just dumb luck?

At one point in the sixteenth century, the pride of Britain's nascent Royal Navy was the warship *Mary Rose*. Launched in 1511, she was retrofitted with heavy cannons designed to fire out of gun ports just a few feet above the water line. In a battle with the French near Portsmouth in 1545, **the ship only got one broadside off before sinking,** taking about 500 men to a watery grave. The disaster is attributed not to enemy fire, but to the *Mary Rose* turning too fast and tipping over so that water poured through the too-low gun ports.

## Rules are rules.

The people of Thailand take their royalty extremely seriously. Just criticizing the royal family can mean fifteen years in prison. In the past, the rules were even more severe. In 1880, when the country was still known as Siam, Queen Consort Sunandha Kumariratana was traveling to one of her palaces when the boat she was in capsized. At the time, **just touching the queen meant the death penalty.** As a result, none of the onlookers helped her, and the queen perished in sight of her terrified subjects.

# They may be pretty, but they're still explosives.

Fireworks displays have been part of human history for centuries. Usually, the festivities go well—but sometimes they end badly, like in Paris in May 1770, at festivities celebrating the recent marriage of Louis, Dauphin of France (later King Louis XVI), and Austrian archduchess Marie-Antoinette with a huge array of fireworks. When the rockets started a fire, the huge crowd panicked. **People were crushed underfoot and drowned in the Seine River.** Death toll estimates range wildly, from 132 to 3,000. But, even at 132 casualties, it remains the deadliest fireworks display in history. The evening's royal celebrants survived, only to be guillotined twenty-three years later.

# Maybe don't build bombs in your basement.

Today, 18 West 11th Street in New York's Greenwich Village is just another multi-million-dollar restored brownstone in a lovingly kept historic neighborhood. But in 1970, it was owned by an advertising executive who didn't realize that, while he was on a Caribbean vacation, his daughter had moved in four friends. All members of the militant anti-war group the Weathermen, they **started building nail bombs in the basement.** On March 6, the dynamite prematurely exploded, killing three of the group. The other two, including the daughter, escaped death but not prison. Dustin Hoffman, who lived next door to the bomb factory, thankfully escaped unharmed.

# Keep your diseases to yourself.

Following the arrival of settlers in the Americas, the so-called "Columbian Exchange" saw an unprecedented amount of culture, food, traditions, and even animals swapped between the Indigenous people and Europeans. There were some positive aspects (like the proliferation of new crops), but the negatives were horrific. **Europeans brought many diseases to which Native Americans had no previous exposure.** A century and a half after Christopher Columbus landed on Hispaniola in 1492, 80 to 95 percent of the native population was dead from imported illnesses. So many died, in fact, that the Europeans compounded the tragedy by bringing enslaved people from Africa to work the crops.

# These anti-aging trends are out of hand.

A fantastic story helps people make sense of an ugly reality. That could apply to Hungarian countess Elizabeth Báthory (1560–1614). Her husband, Count Ferencz Nádasdy, was often away fighting wars. Rumors swirled in his absence about Báthory torturing and murdering young peasant women. Fears of the sadistic "Blood Countess," **thought to bathe in the blood of her virgin victims to stay young,** hit a fever pitch after Nádasdy died in 1604. Arrested in 1609 amid hints she was also killing royals, authorities connected Báthory to over 600 murders. She died in her cell five years later, somewhat disproving the theory she was a vampire.

# Is it too late to move?

When you're in a deadly pandemic, isolation can only keep you safe until you inevitably have to go back out into the world. But public policy where you live can make a big difference in your odds of survival when you do. **During the 1918 influenza pandemic, half a million Americans died in just a few months.** The fatalities were not evenly spread, though. Around the same time St. Louis was closing public spaces, like churches and schools, Philadelphia held a big parade. The death rate from the flu in Philadelphia (748 per 100,000) was over twice that of St. Louis (358 per 100,000). Hopefully the parade was nice.

# When combs could kill.

Celluloid, a flammable but cheap and easily moldable material, was once used to make a lot of things besides film, including combs. A 1901 newspaper story about burned "celluloid comb victims"—women whose combs had combusted—called the items **"a dangerous article of female adornment."** But women weren't the only victims. Eight years later, two workers burned to death after a box of celluloid exploded at a New York comb factory. And in 1910, a man died after his beard was ignited by his celluloid comb. Celluloid has been mostly replaced by other materials—except for in ping-pong balls, which do not appear to be catching fire at an abnormally high rate. Yet.

# No, you would not rather be a horrible warning than a good example.

The enemies of Oliver Cromwell, who died of natural causes in 1658, dug up his corpse three years after his death just to cut off his head and stick it on a spike at the Palace of Westminster so everybody could see. **It probably didn't bother him, being already dead, but others may not have been so lucky.** The earliest archaeological evidence of human skulls being displayed is from 8,000 years ago, and the peculiar tradition spans cultures. Tribes like the Celts were very fond of lopping the heads off their highest-profile enemies and showing them off. With thousands of such displays throughout history, odds are good they weren't all postmortem.

# There are fates worse than jail for a stowaway.

After the cargo ship *Arran* left Scotland for Quebec in 1868, the crew discovered they had stowaways. Seven boys, aged eleven to twenty-two, had snuck on board. Captain Robert Watt and first mate James Kerr **subjected the stowaways to starvation and frequent beatings before forcefully disembarking them onto an ice pack** off Newfoundland. Two of the younger boys, Hugh M'Ewan and Hugh M'Ginnes, died before the rest were rescued. News spread about the marooned "boys on the ice" and, by the time the *Arran* got back to Scotland, an enraged mob was ready to dole out justice. Watt and Kerr were tried and imprisoned for their crimes, which is frankly better than they deserved.

## You always think you'll be the exception.

For centuries, people convicted of capital crimes in Scotland had their heads lopped off by a big guy swinging a sword or axe. Because this was fairly messy and inefficient, the powers that be were happy to switch to the "Maiden" in 1564. **The so-called "Scottish beheading machine" was essentially a ten-foot-tall guillotine.** On June 2, 1581, Scottish authorities used it to separate the head of James Douglas, Earl of Morton, from his body for his complicity in the murder of Henry Stewart, Lord Darnley, second husband to Mary, Queen of Scots. Ironically, Douglas had a hand in introducing the killing machine to Scotland.

## Striking oil isn't all it's cracked up to be.

In 1870, the Osage Nation signed a treaty with the United States, exchanging their Kansas reservation for land in the Oklahoma Territory. The subsequent discovery of oil underneath Osage land in 1894 seemed like good luck. But by the early 1920s, dozens of Osage with profitable headrights (royalties from oil on their property) had **died from inexplicable wasting disease, gunshots, and at least one bomb.** An investigation (and several confessions from partners in crime) revealed William Hale, a non-Osage businessman and wannabe cartoon villain, had orchestrated many of the killings to amass control of the victims' headrights income.

# Either this wallpaper goes, or I do.

By the time Napoleon Bonaparte was imprisoned on the island of Saint Helena, he should have died many times over. Until then, it had been just his soldiers dying—a half-million just from France, a couple million more from armies who fought against him in the many battles he led. Theories have swirled about enemies causing Napoleon's May 5, 1821, death; he had been raving about dying "before [his] time, murdered by the English oligarchy and its assassin." Oddly enough, **it was most likely the arsenic in his wallpaper that did him in.** Back then, arsenic was a common enough ingredient in household goods (not to mention the syphilis treatment Napoleon required).

## SURVIVAL TIP

You would be shocked by how many things in your house can kill you, from radon to mold and carbon monoxide. Luckily, there are monitors, tests, and air purifiers for most of them. One of the best things you can do (besides setting a reminder to change the batteries in those monitors) is increase your home's ventilation. In other words, open the windows now and then.

# Don't underestimate someone with nothing to lose.

Toward the end of World War II, the Japanese Empire saw the writing on the wall. So they turned many of their remaining planes into suicide bombs, of course. Kamikaze pilots in the Special Attack Corps (some volunteers, others coerced) had a special ceremony, drank some sake, and then tried to **smash their explosive-and-gasoline-packed planes into important targets.** Close to 4,000 Japanese pilots were killed, but they took 47 ships and 7,000 U.S., British, and Australian soldiers with them. That's a lot, but it could have been worse; the kamikazes were shot down before hitting their targets 87 percent of the time.

# The odds were not in their favor.

The Soviet Union was known for many things before its fall: propaganda art, grocery stores full of empty shelves, and bad cars, not to mention lots and lots of gulags. These were the hundreds of isolated prison camps where the Soviet leadership banished millions of enemies, both real and imagined. The bitter cold, lack of food, primitive conditions, and brutal punishments meant **roughly 10 percent of prisoners died.** But escape was daunting, mostly due to the gulags' isolation. Two Polish prisoners who somehow evaded capture in 1945 still had to cross over 1,300 miles to get home.

# Just imagine how many duels social media would cause.

Pride was easily wounded in Europe during the Middle Ages, which led to a lot of duels. Generally, this happened when a "gentleman" felt insulted and demanded satisfaction. These one-on-one clashes were highly choreographed ritual combat with swords, and later pistols, that ended when a participant was wounded or killed. And there was usually no legal way out of a duel once someone was officially challenged. For a while, **courts even used "judicial duels" to settle cases,** which certainly saved on legal fees. The contests became so popular that, during one decade in the reign of Henry IV, duels killed about 6,000 people. Thankfully for us, they fell out of favor in the nineteenth century.

# Even peaceful protests can end badly.

One of the most violent protests in American history began with good intentions. In Chicago, on May 3, 1886, several workers had been wounded, and at least two killed, when police tried to break up a fight between striking workers and strikebreakers at the McCormick Reaper Works factory. The next day, May 4, anarchist labor leaders were holding a peaceful protest against police brutality in Haymarket Square when, in a stellar PR move, police tried to forcefully clear the lingering crowd. Then a bomb exploded. **Unable to identify the bomber, police fired their guns at random.** Seven officers and as many as eight civilians were killed, and dozens more were wounded.

# Better safe than assassinated.

Despite the assassinations of two American presidents, President William McKinley had no armed protection at a reception in Buffalo, New York, on September 6, 1901. This meant Leon Czolgosz, a Detroit anarchist who thought McKinley was an "enemy of the people," could walk right up with his revolver. The president took two shots to the chest and was bundled off to the hospital, where he was expected to recover. **Eight days later, he died from gangrene.** (There was obviously some room for improvement in early wound treatments.) Incredibly, McKinley showed no malice toward Czolgosz. One of the first things the president said after being shot was, "Don't hurt him."

# Not all military assignments are created equal.

One thing to remember about joining the military: you generally go where they send you. During World War II, the average British airman might have wanted to stay out of the Royal Air Force's Bomber Command. The 125,000 men who served as aircrew had to fly bombers several hundred miles over enemy territory while German gunners and fighter planes tried to kill them. **Only 54 percent survived**—the worst survival rate of any Allied unit in the war (and that's not including men who were taken as prisoners of war).

# Maybe just a trim?

In the sixteenth century, well before becoming known as the birthplace of Hitler, the Bavarian town of Braunau am Inn boasted something most other places could not: a mayor whose beard was over four and a half feet long. But it brought the well-liked Hans Steininger to an unlikely end on September 28, 1567. Caught in a crowd panicked by fire, **Steininger tripped over his beard, fell down some stairs, and broke his neck.** Before he was buried, his loyal constituents snipped off the beard and preserved it in the town museum, where today, it serves as a warning to overly bearded men.

# You probably had to be there.

Pietro Aretino was precocious from the jump. He left his hometown of Arezzo for Perugia and eventually made his way to Rome, where he gained favor for his propaganda in support of the Pope. But he was eventually forced out because he had offended too many people in high places. Settling in Venice, Aretino made his name as **a blasphemous satirist who profited by blackmailing intended targets of his sharp tongue.** All in all, he seemed to enjoy himself. The most famous story of his death in 1556 (which may or may not have been exaggerated . . . or even true) describes him laughing so hard at a lewd story about his sister that he fell out of his chair and hit his head on the floor.

## Maybe he should have thrown his staff a pizza party.

Sir Fulke Greville of Warwickshire, England, was no slouch when it came to his letters. A counselor to kings, statesman, and knights, he also used much of his time putting pen to paper to create everything from sonnets to tragic dramas and political commentary. Greville's life ended in a far less dignified a manner than he lived it, though. In 1628, **a disgruntled servant fatally stabbed Greville while he was in the toilet** before killing himself. Perhaps suggesting things untold, the grand tomb that Greville designed for himself includes the epitaph *Trophaeum Peccati*, or "Sin's Trophy."

## There's nothing like a grandmother's love.

In the year 24, Roman senator Marcus Plautius Silvanus's wife Apronia fell to her death from their bedroom window—an apparent suicide. But her father didn't buy it. He asked Emperor Tiberius to intervene, which was bad for Silvanus. Tiberius was a wannabe detective before the job existed. He loved investigating things, and Silvanus's story certainly sounded like a cover-up for murder. After examining the scene of the crime and finding evidence of a struggle, Tiberius had Silvanus arrested. He didn't face a trial, though. **Instead, he faced judgment from his grandmother, Urgulania, who sent him a dagger.** The message was clear, but the cold-blooded murderer was suddenly squeamish and had to receive help slitting his wrists.

"One must never
set up a murder.
They must happen
unexpectedly,
as in life."

—ALFRED HITCHCOCK

## Chapter 7

# MURDER MOST STRANGE

# If you're murdered by mistake, the least the killer can do is apologize.

When gangsters wearing police uniforms shot Giulio Giaccio to death in Naples in 2000, they left nothing to chance. **The killers smashed his teeth with a hammer and dissolved his corpse in acid to evade identification.** The only problem was that twenty-six-year-old Giulio wasn't the target. Assassins from the Polverinos, a Neapolitan Camorra crime clan, were looking for somebody else when they mistakenly murdered the young construction worker. After realizing their error—and just before the case went to trial—the Polverinos offered Giulio's family about $32,000 and an apartment to say they were sorry. It takes a big man to dissolve someone in acid. But it takes an even bigger man to admit he was wrong.

## Irony and wrongful convictions know no bounds.

It's the worst nightmare of anyone with a weekly crime procedural on their watchlist: wrongful conviction. Christopher Williams was sent to death row after being convicted of shooting four Philadelphia men to death in 1989. **Years later, a key witness to the killings admitted to having lied.** Williams' sentence was vacated, and he was released in February 2021, after nearly thirty years in prison. Later that year, he rightfully filed a wrongful conviction lawsuit. In December 2022, Williams was fatally shot in the head while attending a funeral for another formerly imprisoned man. Williams' estate settled his lawsuit for $3 million three months later.

# Don't poke the obviously unhinged bear.

As he staggered to his death in 1812, British Prime Minister Spencer Perceval shouted, "I am murdered!" The man who shot him, John Bellingham, waited patiently in the lobby of the British House of Commons to be arrested. He ascribed his reasoning to "want of redress, and denial of justice." A few years before, Bellingham had been imprisoned in Russia over refusing to pay a contested debt. He then became obsessed with the idea that the British government owed him compensation. Instead, they told him to do his worst. So he did. **While he would have preferred to kill Britain's ambassador to Russia, he felt assassinating the Prime Minster was a suitable alternative.** At his murder trial in 1813, Bellingham argued he was justified, saying, "When a minister sets himself above the laws, as Mr. Perceval did, he does it at his own personal risk."

## These one-hit wonders are killer.

If a character in a book or movie killed somebody by hitting them once in the face, audiences would scoff. But so-called "one-punch deaths" are common enough to have led to the formation of the awareness-raising One Punch Can Kill campaign. **Sometimes, a single hit to the head can fatally injure the brain.** Even if the punch itself doesn't kill, it can cause a person to black out and die from hitting their head on pavement or another hard surface. The one-punch threat makes it even clearer that, when facing a belligerent goon, the best response is to just run away.

# What flavors go best with antifreeze?

Two Springfield, Missouri, murders played out like a murder mystery game, with a preacher playing the part of detective. Just before Mark Staudte died in 2012, his friends noticed his slurred speech and his skin's yellow tint. Five months later, Mark's autistic son Shaun died with flu-like symptoms. Both had a ring of blood around their mouths. The next year, Mark's daughter Sarah was hospitalized with organ failure. **The family pastor put the clues together and called the police.** Mark's wife, Diane, and other daughter, Rachel, confessed that they had poisoned their family members by mixing antifreeze with their Coca-Cola and Gatorade to mask the taste. Asked why she killed her son, Diane told police he was "more than a pest."

# The Lainz Angels of Death were not a band.

In 1983, a quartet of nurse's aides at Vienna's Lainz Hospital began murdering their patients, especially the older and infirm. Over the next seven years, Waltraud Wagner, Maria Gruber, Irene Leidolf, and Stefanija Mayer committed somewhere between 49 and upward of 200 murders. **Insulin and tranquilizers were the favored weapons of the aides, who became known as the Lainz Angels of Death.** But these weren't mercy killings. One Angel told Austrian police that patients "who got on [her] nerves were dispatched directly to a free bed with the good Lord."

The Little Book of Horrors

## Just because she was a murderer doesn't mean she was a bad nurse.

In 1981, staff at Texas's Bexar County Hospital noticed that children in the ICU kept dying between 3 p.m and 11 p.m. They called it the "Death Shift." An investigation found that the victims were in the care of one nurse—Genene Jones—but they couldn't prove malpractice. **So, instead, they concocted a layoff and sent a likely serial killer off with a good recommendation.** Jones went on her merry way to a hospital in Kerrville, Texas, where the mysterious deaths continued. Eventually, the "Angel of Death" was caught. While she was convicted of murdering one child, the skilled killer may have murdered as many as sixty. Incredibly, no one thought to suspend her nursing license until two years after her conviction.

## Not everyone is a Good Samaritan.

On October 26, 2001, Gregory Glenn Biggs of Fort Worth, Texas, had the misfortune of finding himself in front of Chante Jawan Mallard's car. High on alcohol, marijuana, and ecstasy, the nurse's aide drove right into Biggs. Instead of doing the normal thing—taking Biggs to the hospital, where his life would almost certainly have been saved—**Mallard drove home with the man embedded in her windshield and left him there to die in her garage.** The defense attorney argued that Mallard was "not a horrible person," but the judge didn't see it that way. They sentenced her to fifty years in prison for murder, and another ten for tampering with evidence.

# Dating is murder.

Dating apps are just the latest in a long line of disappointing ways to meet people. Once upon a time, there were these things called "personal ads," which helped people make love connections via newsprint (e.g., "Gregarious Gemini, 35, seeks vigorous Virgo"). The ads were sometimes also a conduit for murder. **Most cases involved men preying on women, but there were exceptions.** Enter: Belle Gunness. She started her killing career in Chicago around 1900, likely poisoning her husband and infant children for the insurance money. Afterward, Gunness settled on an Indiana farm and placed classified ads for a would-be husband. Men arrived with their life savings, then disappeared. When the farm burned down in 1908, authorities discovered the remains of more than forty victims, including those of her suitors and even some children. Gunness, however, had ghosted them.

### SURVIVAL TIP

Rule number one of online dating: always meet in a public place (i.e., not at a remote farm, residence, or alleyway). Tell friends where you're going. Keep your phone handy. If the vibes are off, get away fast; possible embarrassment beats the alternative. Of course, a pre-date background check never hurts, either.

# "Nice inn, just a little murdery."

Weary travelers on Kansas's Osage Trail in the 1870s might have been happy to find the family-run Bender Inn. It was a popular spot because of Kate Bender, a pretty young woman known for faith healing and free love. But a missing persons investigation in 1873 led searchers to a horrifying scene. The inn had been turned into a blood-soaked and body part–strewn charnel house. As it turns out, the mysterious Benders—who were never captured, were not a family, were probably not named Bender, and killed a lot of people—**would seat their victims at the dinner table, knock them out with a hammer, slit their throats, and drop them through a trap door.** Several lucky travelers fled, but nearly twenty bodies were found on the property. (This is why we need TripAdvisor.)

# Teenagers are terrifying.

Unlike what B-movies would have us believe, the original so-called "thrill killers" were not drug-crazed hippie bikers. They were a quartet of Brooklyn teenagers who came up with a disturbing way of entertaining themselves in the summer of 1954. Jack Koslow, Melvin Mittman, Jerome Lieberman, and Robert Trachtenberg roamed the streets restlessly, assaulting, beating, and torturing women and vagrants. They even threatened to set some on fire. The gang killed two men, one of whom they drowned by hurling him into the East River. **The public blamed the pointless crimes on the combination of impressionable youth and violent comic books,** which was a novel approach to criminology.

# Family trauma will catch up to you.

A serial criminal with an abusive father and a mentally ill mother, Danny Rolling started taking his trauma out on others in his teens. At 35, he murdered three members of a family in Shreveport, Louisiana, after getting fired from his job. The following year, he shot and wounded his father—a veteran cop— before moving to Florida under a new identity. And over three days in August of 1990, **he killed and mutilated five University of Florida students, leaving the head of one victim on a shelf.** One woman heard the news and called the tip line, recounting how Rolling once told her husband he liked to "stick knives into people" (something she may have wanted to mention to authorities sooner). But it wasn't until Rolling was jailed for an unrelated burglary that police discovered they'd nabbed the Gainesville Ripper.

# Watch what you eat.

Unlike many serial killers, Carl Grossmann combined his murderous pastime with his day job (not an easy task). Grossman lived in Berlin, Germany, where he sold meat on the black market during World War I and, later, owned a hot dog stand. In his spare time, **authorities believe he lured dozens of women (some of them his employees, others homeless or prostitutes) to their death in his apartment,** where he brutally butchered them. In a *Sweeney Todd* twist, many believe he was using his street catering services as a way to dispose of his victims' bodies.

# Even good guys have their limits.

Most people in the small East Texas town of Carthage liked Bernie Tiede, the nice mortician who sang in the choir and had a kind word for everyone. They felt less favorably toward Marjorie Nugent, the reclusive millionaire widow who rarely had a kind word for anyone. When Tiede became Nugent's companion and caretaker, people found it odd. When nobody saw Nugent for months, they found it suspicious. **And when police discovered her body stashed in one of her own freezers in 1997, people made excuses.** One woman even warned the prosecutor that Nugent "was so mean that even if Bernie did kill her, you won't be able to find anyone in town who's going to convict him." But Tiede confessed to shooting the old battle-ax and went to prison anyway.

# From the pig's intestine to your medicine cabinet.

Heparin is basically a good thing. It's a kind of anticoagulant, or blood thinner, which is used to minimize the risk of blood clots during dialysis and heart surgeries. But it can also have a long and unmonitored supply chain. In 2008, **approximately 150 deaths in the United States were linked to a contaminated supply of heparin,** the base material for which is harvested from pig intestines in China. But the pigs weren't the problem. The drug wound its way through a dizzying maze of often unregulated middlemen and subcontractors—one of whom added a toxic ingredient to cut costs—before ending up in the veins of patients who, quite reasonably, assumed it was safe to take.

# The cure can be worse
# than the disease.

In the fall of 1982, at least seven people in the Chicago suburbs died mysteriously. Soon, authorities discovered a link: the deceased had all taken Tylenol before passing away. An investigation found that **the pain medication had been dosed with cyanide** somewhere between the factory and the purchase point. They never found the culprit, but we have them to thank for that "tamper-proof" foil on pill bottles that is so hard to punch through when you have a headache. Tylenol spent over $100 million on a massive recall and safety measures to prevent mass poisoning.

# Remote cabins are horror-movie
# fodder for a reason.

What happens if someone is killed in the woods, and no one is around to hear it? Movie writers make up their own ending. On April 12, 1981, poor fourteen-year-old Sheila Sharp returned from a sleepover to find the tied-up bodies of her mother, her brother, and his friend in their small cabin in the remote northern California town of Keddie. **Vicious knife and hammer wounds left blood everywhere.** The skull of Sheila's twelve-year-old sister would be found in the woods fifty miles away three years later. And somehow, Sheila's two little brothers and one of their friends in another room slept through it all. Leads have come and gone, but the killers have yet to be caught, which is probably why movies like *The Strangers* have stepped in to fill in the blanks.

# A citrusy bouquet, with notes of death.

The two Russian agents who disembarked the Aeroflot flight to London in 2018 seemed like normal guys. That was, until they traveled about 85 miles to Salisbury, where **they sprayed a man's door with perfume and nearly killed him.** The GRU officers had retrofitted a perfume bottle into a delivery system for the deadly nerve agent Novichok. (You might recognize the name from the attempted murder of late Russian dissident Aleksei Navalny.) The door belonged to Sergei Skripal—a former GRU colonel turned double agent for England's MI6. Later that day, Skripal, his daughter, and the investigating police officer were all hospitalized. They recovered, but one unlucky woman who spritzed the discarded poison on her wrists died.

# Poisoned by your own cat-meat stew.

Three guys getting together in the southern Chinese city of Yangjiang over some cat-meat stew (a local delicacy) in 2011 was nothing unusual. But when they were all hospitalized, authorities became suspicious. Local official Huang Guang, they discovered, had dropped *Gelsemium elegans* into the stew of one of his dining companions, wealthy businessman Long Liyuan, over an embezzlement accusation. **The rare poisonous herb, known as "heartbreak grass" and favored by your more refined Chinese assassins-for-hire, did Long in.** Like a villain in a spy movie, Huang endured some of the tainted stew to throw suspicion off himself. (It didn't work.)

# That cuppa tea could be your last.

Alexander Litvinenko, the ex-KGB agent turned Vladimir Putin critic, had tea in London in 2006 with a couple Russians he thought were prospective business partners. They were actually agents looking to take him out. The killers dosed their target's tea with polonium-210. **The incredibly lethal radioactive element sent Litvinenko to the hospital and, after a few agonizing weeks, the grave.** But the most remarkable part of the story is that the killers lived to tell the tale (or *not* tell it). They had been spectacularly sloppy, spreading the easily traced polonium-210 everywhere they went in London. That included a bordello-themed club whose decor included a bronze phallus, but authorities made sure to note that "no polonium was found on the phallus."

# It was the cop who done it.

On a hot New York summer morning in July 1912, two-bit bookie Herman Rosenthal stepped out onto 43rd Street and was gunned down by a quartet of gangsters. Rosenthal's offense wasn't refusing to pay a winning bet, or even getting on the gangsters' bad sides. **His fatal mistake was accusing police lieutenant Charles Becker of demanding kickbacks.** Rosenthal was right, but what nerve! Incensed by the charge, Becker hired the gunmen to shut the bookie's mouth. The killers and Becker were executed in the electric chair, but that didn't help Rosenthal.

## Being eaten dead is better than being eaten alive.

The line "ate her piece by piece" in the Rolling Stones' "Too Much Blood" sounds sexy until you learn that it's about Issei Sagawa—aka the "Kobe Cannibal." While studying literature in Paris in 1981, **Sagawa murdered fellow student Renée Hartevelt, ate part of her body, and disposed of the rest of it in Bois de Boulogne park.** Although Sagawa's guilt was largely undisputed (he talked openly about killing and consuming Hartevelt), jurisdictional tangles kept the Japanese citizen out of prison. At one point, he even became a Japanese TV celebrity. But once his fifteen minutes were over, he found it surprisingly hard to make a living as a known murderer.

## Worst game ever.

If you've got trust issues when it comes to romantic relationships, you may want to skip this one. In 2020, Floridian Sarah Boone was charged with murder after her boyfriend, Jorge Torres Jr., was found dead and heavily bruised. **Boone had zipped him into a suitcase, allegedly in a game of hide-and-seek gone wrong.** The Florida State Attorney's office released footage they said was from Boone's cellphone of a conversation between her and Torres. At one point, Torres is heard saying he couldn't breathe. Boone, laughing, replies, "That's on you."

## That's not what they meant by "killing time."

The food, the boredom, the unflattering clothing—prison is obviously not fun. But maybe that's for the best when even playing a low-stakes game can get you killed. In 2001, Christopher Newton and his cellmate Jason Brewer were having a nice game of chess when things went haywire. Supposedly frustrated that Brewer kept quitting each time the game went badly for him, **Newton strangled the sore loser to death.** (There's an encouragement technique chess academies have yet to try.) He later admitted that another prisoner had hired him to assault Brewer, but that inmate didn't ask Newton to drink Brewer's blood, which he did.

## If they'll kill with you, they'll kill you.

By the 1980s, Anthony "Tony the Ant" Spilotro had worn out a lot of good will. An ambitious member of the Outfit (the Chicago Mafia), Spilotro had done many murders in the 1960s. That was fine with the Outfit; those were approved. Then Spilotro was sent to Las Vegas on some Outfit business, which eventually ended in more murders. And as fans of *Casino* know, that didn't sit well with the elders. (Think Joe Pesci, aka Nicky Santoro. Sound familiar?) As punishment, enforcers lured Spilotro and his brother (and fellow Outfit member) Michael to a Chicago basement and beat them to death. Why both? Because, as associate Frank Cullotta said: **"If you whack one, you gotta whack them both."**

# Don't take vodka
# from strangers.

Murdering people is bad enough, but using the memory of your dead dog to do it is a new low. Alexander Pichushkin seemed harmless enough when asking strangers in Moscow to share a bottle of vodka in grief over losing his beloved pup. Little did they know he had a dark ulterior motive: **a plan to murder sixty-four people, one for every square on a chessboard.** Called the "Chessboard Killer" (a descriptive if unoriginal moniker) as well as the "Maniac," he ultimately fell short of his goal, eventually admitting to killing sixty people. His method of choice was often a hammer to the head, but he would also thrust the neck of the vodka bottle into the wound for good measure.

## SURVIVAL TIP

Most people wouldn't think twice about stopping to chat with an elderly woman or pick a flyer off their windshield. And that's how they get you. Killers and traffickers use all kinds of tricks and accomplices to distract unwary victims. Stay aware of your surroundings at all times. Most importantly, never let an attacker (or would-be attacker) take you to a second location.

## Generational wealth cuts
## both ways.

Chester and Clara Congdon made a fortune mining in northern
Minnesota, and they proudly built a grand lakeside mansion in
Duluth in 1909. By 1977, it belonged to their last living daughter,
83-year-old Elisabeth. Little did Elisabeth know, one of her adopted
daughters, **Marjorie, was blowing through her trust fund
and counting on an $8 million inheritance that seemed
too far off.** When an intruder murdered Elisabeth and her night
nurse, Velma Pietila, with a candlestick, Marjorie was the obvious
suspect. But her husband Roger was the one to confess and serve
time. Marjorie eventually went to prison, too, but for arson, not
murder—despite being linked to *several* mysterious deaths.

## Where'd all the serial
## killers go?

According to the kind of not-easily-spooked researchers who
study this sort of thing, the peak serial-killer era spanned the
1970s through the 1980s. Fewer people appear to be getting
killed in sprees these days, which is a good thing. But that drop
has suspiciously coincided with **a drop in the number of
homicide cases solved by police from 91 percent to
a disquieting 61.6 percent**. A 2019 article in *The Atlantic*
suggests serial killers are now better at evading the law and
quotes one expert who thinks there are up to 4,000 of them
operating in the United States. So lock those doors!

# Bad seeds grow in the most likely places.

It was a hard-knock life for Hannah Ocuish, who was born into poverty in Connecticut in 1773 with a mental disability and spent her childhood bouncing around wealthy homes as an indentured servant. Ocuish had her first brush with authorities at age six, when she and her older brother robbed and beat a young girl. **At age twelve, she was hanged for murder.** Accused of stealing strawberries by Eunice Bolles, the six-year-old daughter of a wealthy family, Ocuish had spent weeks plotting her revenge. When locals discovered Bolles' mangled body by the road, Ocuish offered a tearful confession. It earned her no mercy. She was hanged that December and remains the youngest person ever executed in American history.

# Good help is hard to find.

Delores Gillespie was a seventy-three-year-old Brooklynite beloved by her neighbors. Thinking she needed help around her apartment, she hired Jerome Isaac to give her a hand. The arrangement turned bad after she discovered Isaac had been stealing. **Fuming after being caught and fired, the thief plotted revenge against his former employer.** On December 17, 2011, Isaac cornered Gillespie in the elevator, quickly spraying her with an accelerant before throwing a firebomb that burned the poor woman to death. When Isaac turned himself in to the police, his face was badly burned, and he still smelled of gasoline.

# Spiked drinks: an elementary way to die.

When Manchester, England, businessman John Fletcher was found dead an hour after hailing a cab in 1889, police were stumped. Fletcher had been robbed, but there were no signs of violence, just alcohol and the insomnia drug chloral hydrate in his system. **Shrewdly, they called on one of the century's great detectives and the inspiration for Sherlock Holmes: Jerome Caminada.** He connected the death to two other cases, a recent theft of the drug and its use in illegal prizefighting, to arrest boxer Charlie Parton. The final piece of the puzzle was a witness who saw the soon-to-be convict spike Fletcher's drink in a pub, causing a lethal interaction, before the victim took his last cab ride.

# Successful entrepreneur wasn't on the menu.

In the 1990s, Sushil Sharma and his wife Naina Sahni were something of a power couple in Delhi, India. Sharma was a youth leader for India's then-monolithic Congress Party. Sahni was also a Congress Party member, as well as a licensed pilot and boutique owner. But appearances can be deceiving. Jealous over Sahni's friendship with a colleague, Sharma shot and killed her in July 1995. **He contemplated throwing his wife's body in the river, but there was traffic on the bridge.** So instead, he convinced a friend who managed a local restaurant to help him dispose of her. Alerted by a vendor who thought the restaurant was on fire, a police constable discovered the men fanning the tandoor oven with Sahni's body sticking out of it. The fire's fuel? Congress Party posters.

# Unsolved murders make for good podcasts and poor sleep.

In September 1982, fishermen in Craig, Alaska, noticed commercial fishing boat *The Investor* on fire in the harbor. They then watched a man arrive at the dock in the boat's skiff, coolly offer it to anyone who wanted to get a closer look, and walk away. **Once the fire was under control, police found eight bodies on board:** the owner, Mark Coulthurst, his pregnant wife, their 4-year-old son and 5-year-old daughter and four teenage deckhands, all shot to death in their bunks two days earlier. But without a suspect or a motive, the state's largest mass murder remains unsolved and keeping Alaskans in the previously peaceful village up at night.

# There are fates worse than death.

Their love story was like something out of a movie—namely, *Fatal Attraction*. Dutch engineer Mark van Dongen was working in the United Kingdom in 2010 when he fell for Berlinah Wallace. After they broke up in 2015, Wallace began harassing Van Dongen. And in September of that year, she said, "If I can't have you, no one else will" before dousing him with sulfuric acid. **The brutal attack left him horribly scarred, mostly paralyzed and blind, and unable to care for himself.** Depressed and desperate for relief from agonizing pain, Van Dongen was moved to Belgium to be with his father and apply for humane euthanasia. He died in January 2017 at the age of twenty-nine. A year later, Wallace was sentenced to life in prison, although she could be eligible for parole after twelve years.

> *"Life is hard. Then you die. Then they throw dirt in your face. Then the worms eat you. Be grateful if it happens in that order."*
> **—DAVID GERROLD**

## This isn't what they mean by "a little off the top."

Florence, Montana (population: 901), was never a hotbed of criminal activity. And November 6, 2001, was an ordinary day for town salon the Hair Gallery, where an employee was peacefully giving a woman a manicure. **Then a man came in, shoved the two into a closet, and cut their throats.** Not long after, the salon owner came in and met the same terrible end. The killer was never found, and rumors of drug debts and assassins swirled. But one detail stands out: a witness saw the killer wearing a trench coat and a stovepipe hat. So, you can't fully rule out time travel.

## A ride-by shooting with flair.

Although Latin America's drug kingpins get all the credit when it comes to grisly murders, the "Godmother of cocaine" was no slouch. Colombia's queenpin Griselda Blanco ran much of Miami's booming cocaine trade in the late 1970s and early 1980s. **She cemented her reign with dozens of murders, including a two-year-old child and probably all three of her husbands.** Her preferred method of death-dealing was the motorcycle drive-by. Fittingly, after serving nearly two decades in American prison, she was shot dead in Medellin by an assassin on a motorcycle.

# Good parenting can go terribly wrong.

In 1954, teenage best friends Juliet Hulme and Pauline Parker lived in a mutual fantasy world they never wanted to leave. But that dream was shattered when Hulme's parents divorced, and she was told she would have to leave New Zealand to live with an aunt in South Africa. The girls devised a plan: Parker would come with Hulme. But when Parker's mother, Honora, refused, the two crafted a second plan: **bludgeon Honora to death with a stocking-wrapped brick.** Upon being released from prison five years later, the girls assumed new identities. Hulme moved to the United Kingdom, became Anne Perry, and went on to write popular crime novels. As they say, write what you know.

# If you accidentally walk into a mob-run restaurant, walk back out.

For reasons unknown to most, popular culture tends to make mobsters, if not lovable, then at least likable (see: everything from *Analyze This* to *The Sopranos*). **But, in reality, gangsters are some of the most consistently dangerous people in the world.** According to a 2019 United Nations report, between 2000 and 2017, street gangs and organized crime groups caused more deaths than all the armed conflicts raging during that period (and there were *a lot*). Although the famous gangsters of Japan and Italy get most of the notoriety, the majority of mobster killings take place in the Caribbean and Latin America.

# Envy kills.

On December 8, 1980, John Lennon was no longer a Beatle, but he seemed in an optimistic mood. He was on better terms with his former bandmates and had just released (with his wife Yoko Ono) the album *Double Fantasy*, which went multi-platinum and won a Grammy. But on that day, **Lennon was shot dead by a deranged and envious fan** just outside his Upper West Side apartment building. He had given a radio interview just hours earlier in which he said, "I consider that my work won't be finished until I'm dead and buried, and I hope that's a long, long time."

## Vending-machine fare has always been iffy.

In April 1985, Japanese psychologists created a term for a new breed of remorseless killer who found satisfaction in victims' suffering—*yukaihan*. The unusual series of killings that inspired it started with a truck driver who died after drinking a bottle of herbicide-poisoned juice left on top of a vending machine. (Why he drank discarded juice is its own mystery.) **The vending-machine poisonings continued, killing twelve people and sickening thirty-five more.** But they stopped suddenly after the twelfth fatality: a teenage girl who was the only female killed. Whether the *yukaihan* moved on or only wanted to target men, no one knows. They were never caught.

# Wedgies can hurt more than feelings.

Fights between adults are rarely pretty but, while stupid, are usually nonfatal. Yet there are exceptions. On December 21, 2013, thirty-year-old Oklahoman and former Marine Brad Lee Davis got into a confrontation with his fifty-eight-year-old stepfather, Denver St. Clair, in the latter's trailer. It ended with Davis giving St. Clair an atomic wedgie. (For the non-bullies or -bullied, that's where you pull someone's underwear over their head from behind.) **Instead of simply embarrassing the older man, the elastic band from St. Clair's underwear strangled him.** Davis was charged with manslaughter and sentenced to thirty years.

# Maybe video games *are* rotting their brains.

Police in Fayette, Alabama, didn't have any reason for concern when they arrested eighteen-year-old Devin Moore on June 7, 2003. The teen had no record and was only wanted for car theft. But, unbeknownst to the police, Moore had been binge-playing *Grand Theft Auto* for months. Just as he would in the game, **Moore grabbed a pistol from an officer and used it to shoot him dead,** along with another officer and an emergency dispatcher, before driving off in a police cruiser. After his arrest, Moore told police "Life is a video game; everybody has to die sometime."

# Don't role play. Wait, role play!

During the 1980s, some adults believed one of the many threats facing American teens was *Dungeons & Dragons*. According to panicked news coverage, teens who indulged in the fantasy role-playing game were more likely to commit murder or suicide than their peers. But a researcher who dug into the numbers found out **D&D players were actually *not as likely* to kill themselves or others** than their less nerdy counterparts. It's unclear what those more murderous teens were into that made them so dangerous, but clearly they should have been spending more time throwing dice and killing imaginary monsters in their parents' basements.

## Time to look for a different line of work.

During the 1980s, cattle houses in Missouri noticed a weird pattern: several men had bought cattle with checks that later bounced. The cops failed to find the men, many of them transient farmhands working for elderly couple Ray and Faye Copeland in Mooresville. Then, in 1989, they caught a break. Jack McCormick called a crime hotline to say he had escaped from the Copeland farm after Ray had him write a bad check for cattle and then tried to silence him with a rifle. **Five bodies were later dug up near the farm, and the Copelands were sentenced to death.** *The New York Times* referred to the grisly scheme as "rural intrigue."

# Exercise caution in your movie recommendations.

Allan Menzies was your average twenty-two-year-old Scotsman, minus his obsession with the movie adaptation of Anne Rice's novel *Queen of the Damned*. Menzies had seen the film over a hundred times and was convinced the movie's vampire protagonist Akasha was speaking to him and promising him immortality. In 2002, Menzies stabbed and bludgeoned his friend Thomas McKendrick to death for having the audacity to disparage Akasha. **Menzies then drank some of some of his unlucky friend's blood for good measure.** Ironically, McKendrick was the one who introduced Menzies to the movie in the first place.

# Always assume the gun is loaded.

You might think that Bruce Lee's son Brandon Lee being killed by live gunfire on a film set in 1993 would have been the end of using real guns in movies. But no. While rehearsing a scene during the filming of the Western film *Rust* in New Mexico in 2021, **a revolver held by Alec Baldwin fired a live round, killing the cinematographer.** The film's armorer was convicted of involuntary manslaughter over two years later, and arguments have followed about where Baldwin was responsible as well. In the meantime, the practice of using actual guns in films bewilderingly continues.

# Cut off one head, and three grow back.

Up until around 2000, Mexican drug cartels were considered a large but potentially manageable problem. When the long-dominant Institutional Revolutionary Party (PRI) was voted out that year, the new government started waging war on the cartels. Then, in 2006, the military started killing or imprisoning cartel bosses. While a seemingly good idea, this ricocheted with horrible impact. **The cartels fractured into smaller, harder-to-fight, and far more violent factions.** Since then, Mexico has seen a staggering 360,000-plus homicides, plus an escalation in corruption and trafficking, largely due to the cartels. The lesson here: don't pick a fight with ruthless murderers.

# Beware the wendigo.

In March 1879, a Cree man named Swift Runner showed up at a Catholic mission north of Edmonton, Canada, with a horrifying story. He said his nine-person family, who were living in the woods, had starved to death due to the poor hunting season. But Swift Runner later admitted to murdering and eating his family. **He claimed he'd been possessed by a mythological cannibalistic spirit that some tribes called a "wendigo."** Incredibly, this defense didn't fly. Swift Runner was hanged later that year. But he left a legacy—today, the American Psychological Association's list of syndromes includes "wendigo psychosis," which is "characterized by delusions of becoming possessed by a flesh-eating monster." There's something to speak to your therapist about.

# Wear the life vest.

Every spring, Vincent Viafore and his fiancée Angelika Graswald went kayaking on the Hudson River. In 2015, their tradition ended with Graswald calling 9-1-1, saying Viafore's kayak had capsized in rough, frigid water and he had drowned. **Investigators thought it was weird that, while they were searching for his body, Graswald was literally doing cartwheels on social media.** So they weren't surprised to discover she had removed a connector ring from her fiancé's paddle and the drain plug from the kayak. Charged with second-degree murder, Graswald eventually pled guilty to manslaughter and served just three years in prison. Why so little time? Because Viafore chose not to wear a life vest.

## SURVIVAL TIP

If you are plunged into freezing water, your odds of survival are exponentially better if you're wearing a life jacket. But even then, you still have less than 10 minutes before going into shock. It's crucial to stay calm, control your breathing, and get out of the water fast. If you can't, conserve your body heat until you can be rescued by curling into the fetal position with your head above water.

# The dating apps aren't the problem.

It didn't look good for Levi Weeks, who was accused of murdering his rumored fiancée Elma Sands and throwing her body down a well. Sands had moved to Manhattan to work in her cousin's shop when she met Weeks, who lived in the same Greenwich Village boarding house. On December 22, Sands told another cousin she and Weeks were planning to elope. On January 2, Sands' body was discovered, and Weeks was charged with murder. **The year was 1799, and it was young America's first sensational trial.** But Weeks found a team of star lawyers, including Aaron Burr and Alexander Hamilton. Despite their own murderous differences, they got him acquitted.

# Twitchy ghost hunters probably shouldn't be armed.

In 1803, villagers in Hammersmith, England, started whispering about a ghost that rose out of the church graveyard to spook and even assault people late at night. Rumor had it that one woman even died of fright. A posse was formed to see if this "ghost" was just some jerk in a sheet. Unfortunately for Thomas Milwood, he chose to wear white while walking home on the night of January 3, 1804, and **was shot dead by a terrified volunteer.** Later, villager John Graham came forward to confess that he'd dressed up as the ghost to take revenge on some men who had annoyed him. (This is what's known as the "Scooby-Doo ending.")

# Some people are just genetically predisposed to murder.

There is a memorial in the Belanglo State Forest in New South Wales, Australia, to seven backpackers murdered there. Each of the doomed adventurers had been hitchhiking from Sydney to Melbourne between 1989 and 1992 when they met Ivan Milat, a **mustachioed weapons enthusiast and serial criminal.** He was convicted for the killings in 1996 after being identified by escaped would-be victim Paul Onions. In 2012, seventeen-year-old Matthew Milat, a great-nephew of Ivan's, was convicted for axe-murdering a friend in Belanglo while a companion recorded the killing. "That's what the Milats do," Matthew later said.

# Smoking cigarettes can lead to . . . murder?

In the early 1900s, secondhand smoke wasn't the most pressing reason to avoid smokers. A spate of killings had been attributed to the habit. Take sixteen-year-old Charles Cross, for example. Adopted by a printer needing somebody to do chores, the young smoker was charged in 1899 with raping the printer's wife and beating her to death with a shovel. **Cross was described as a "cigarette fiend," which, at the time, was thought to cause insanity.** According to so-called experts, regular smoking "sap[ped] the moral and mental life of its devotee." The defense didn't work for Cross, who was hanged the following year.

# Aim a little higher.

Joan Vollmer was an unheralded linchpin of the 1940s Beatnik clique of Jack Kerouac, Allen Ginsberg, and William S. Burroughs, eventually marrying Burroughs. After brushes with the law for drug-related crimes, the couple set up house in Mexico City. During a drunken party there, Burroughs, a gun enthusiast, asked Vollmer to put a glass on her head so he could practice his "William Tell" routine. **The poor woman died, unsurprisingly, from a bullet to the forehead.** Burroughs was arrested but fled Mexico before he could be tried. In later interviews, he would claim that killing Vollmer made him a writer. (While Vollmer supported Burroughs's art, if asked, she might have considered the price too steep.)

# Being famous is a serious safety risk.

The twentieth century's biggest media circus kicked off on March 1, 1932, when twenty-month-old "Charlie" Lindbergh, Jr. was kidnapped from the home of his parents, writer Anne Morrow Lindbergh and aviator Charles Lindbergh. (Sadly, this wasn't uncommon—there were roughly 3,000 kidnappings for ransom across the country in 1932 that *didn't* make history.) Ransom notes followed, demanding large sums, and the Lindberghs paid one for $50,000 to no avail. **Charlie was found close to the Lindbergh home, killed by a blow to the head.** In 1936, Bruno Hauptmann was electrocuted for the murder. Hauptmann's last statement read, in part, "I am glad that my life in a world which has not understood me has ended."

# No area with a spooky haunted tower is "safe."

The Fox Tower in Beijing, China, has long been considered haunted, and Pamela Werner's 1937 murder certainly didn't help its grim reputation. Werner often bicycled home past the infamous "Badlands" district, assuring friends that "Peking is the safest city in the world." But the adopted teenaged daughter of a British diplomat was found at the base of the tower, **dismembered, drained of blood, and missing organs.** Her pricey platinum-and-diamond watch, however, remained on her wrist. The investigation looked at the decadent European expatriate community, a shadowy sex cult, an angry beau, and a possible politically motivated assassination but failed to catch Pamela's killer.

# That last step's a doozy!

Louis "Lepke" Buchalter started out ripping off pushcarts on New York's Lower East Side. But he had larger ambitions. Teaming up with Jacob "Gurrah" Shapiro, the two built a formidable kickback, extortion, bootlegging, and drug-dealing business. In 1933, Buchalter started Murder, Inc., an assassination-for-profit corporation whose associates (including Bugsy Siegel) carried out as many as a thousand hits. One of those killers, Abe Reles, later turned states' evidence against his bosses. But, in 1941, **Reles mysteriously fell out of his hotel room window despite the presence of police guards,** who must have been looking the other way at the time.

> *"There are horrors beyond life's edge that we do not suspect, and once in a while man's evil prying calls them just within our range."*
> —H. P. LOVECRAFT

## Just don't pick up hitchhikers.

Aileen Wuornos came to serial murder later in life than most,, first killing at the age of thirty-four in 1989. She had survived an abusive childhood before building up a checkered past that included DUIs, prostitution, armed robbery, attempted suicide, and beating up her senior citizen husband. **She killed seven victims in total, all men who picked her up on the highway,** and claimed self-defense. To be fair, the first man was actually a convicted rapist. But before her 2002 execution, Wuornos declared she just hated men and said of her crimes, "And I'd do it again, too."

## The drifters weren't the killers.

Travis Boyd was hitchhiking near San Antonio when he and several other drifters were picked up by Walter Wesley Ellebracht. They couldn't have known that Ellebracht and his son, Junior, had been **kidnapping and enslaving transients** throughout the early 1980s. The father and son duo, who one neighbor described as, "happy people who just like to have a good time," tortured their captives. They also forced them to help imprison and torture more victims and, oddly, to make small wooden keychains. Then Boyd got away and called the police, who found the charred bones of a murdered man and audio recordings of his torture, ending the family business.

"Those who
welcome death
have only
tried it from
the ears up."

—WILSON MIZNER

## Chapter 8

# CULTS AND OTHER CREEPY THINGS

# Which is scarier: alien reptiles or people who believe in them?

In 2017, New Jersey man Steven Mineo was found dead after being shot in the head. Police arrested his girlfriend, Barbara Rogers, who said that Mineo told her to do it. In reality, both had been following the teachings of Sherry Shriner, **a self-proclaimed "Messenger of the Most High God" who thinks reptilian aliens are impersonating people** in a long-term, diabolical world takeover plot. Shriner allegedly told Mineo that Rogers was a "vampire demon," after which Mineo determined Shriner herself was a secret reptile. What led to Mineo's death, only Rogers knows. But her version of the truth is . . . dubious.

# At least their tastebuds were firing on all cylinders.

Under the leadership of "Ti" and "Do," Heaven's Gate members followed a mix of Biblical prophecy and UFO theology since the early 1970s. By 1997, **the group believed the passing Hale-Bopp comet was trailed by a UFO,** which would help them advance to the next level of human evolution—if they could get to it. The members were primed for this after years of trained obedience and a steady diet of science fiction (*The X-Files*, *Star Trek*). The bodies of thirty-nine cult members were found at their San Diego mansion, after they had committed suicide by ingesting phenobarbital (mixed with applesauce to mask the bitter taste).

> *"The difference between a cult and a religion
> is one outlasts its leader."*
> —RAKESH KHURANA

## Delusional minds think alike.

Rod Ferrell became obsessed with the role-playing game *Vampire: The Masquerade* as a teenager in rural Kentucky during the 1990s. He began saying he, himself, was a 500-year-old vampire known as Vesago and gathered other teens around him who called themselves the Vampire Clan. In 1996, the clan **brutally killed the innocent parents of a fifteen-year-old they wanted to induct into the cult.** Ferrell was originally put on death row but later had his sentence changed to life in prison, providing him with much more time for role-playing.

## See, even salad can kill you.

The biggest bioterror attack in American history happened in 1984 and almost nobody remembers it. A few years earlier, several thousand followers of a cult started in India by the bearded mystic Bhagwan Shree Rajneesh in the 1970s built a community, called Rajneeshpuram, in a remote part of Oregon. In a bold move to control local politics, the Rajneeshees decided to sway a 1984 election in their favor by **poisoning salad bars at local restaurants with salmonella.** Over 700 people were sickened. Nobody died, but it might have kept a generation of Oregon kids off vegetables forever.

# One crazy guy can start a war.

Being near China's Taiping Rebellion in the 1850s was a good way to end up dead. It was spurred by an uprising led by Hong Xiuquan. After **feverish visions told him he was Emperor of China and the brother of Jesus Christ,** Hong started a cult called the God Worshipping Society. Hong's "Heavenly Kingdom" was crushed by imperial forces, but he beat them to the punch by dying before being captured (sources vary as to whether his cause of death was food poisoning or suicide). His enemies then dug up his corpse, burned it, and blasted his ashes out of a cannon. They might have been upset about the 20 million or so Chinese who died in the war.

# This isn't what they signed up for.

The thing about cults is, they never *call* themselves cults. When Jim Jones first started his People's Temple in Indianapolis in 1954, he seemed like a decent preacher. Jones's brand of socially conscious Christianity was unusually devoted to racial equality in the pre-civil rights Midwest. The group got bigger but also weirder as **Jones descended into addiction and paranoia.** Twenty-three years later, over 900 people—mostly Temple members—died at Jones' final hideout in Guyana in what was called a mass suicide but later seemed more like mass murder. (Those who didn't willingly drink the cyanide-laced Flavor Aid were injected with it.)

# You say "cult" like it's a bad thing.

Initiates into the Order of the Solar Temple should have had some clues that things would end poorly. The cult—er, "order"—claimed to be a latter-day version of the secret medieval Knights Templar (ding), believed the apocalypse was nigh (ding, ding), and was really interested in "transiting" to another plane of existence (infinite dings). All this culminated in **multiple mass murders and suicides across Europe and Canada in the mid-1990s** that left seventy-four people dead. Remember: If you start wondering, "Am I in a cult?", chances are you already know the answer.

# Martyr, lemming—same difference.

Even fans of obscure early Christian sects may never have heard of the Circumcellions. These fun-loving fanatics roamed northern Africa in the fourth century, promoting then-radical ideas like ending slavery. Unfortunately, they also loved martyrdom and **took to attacking random people with giant clubs** to achieve it. If the rampaging radicals couldn't provoke the stranger into killing them, they would seal the deal on their own by leaping off the nearest cliff. If you saw a Circumcellion coming, the best thing to do was to steer clear and avoid places that would attract jumping martyrs.

# These magicians weren't asking for volunteers.

At worst, the college students thronging Texas' South Padre Island during spring break expect to suffer a wicked hangover. But in 1989, Texas college student Mark Kilroy disappeared after he and his friends crossed into Mexico. A media frenzy spurred a search. The bodies of Kilroy and many others were found at a remote ranch outside Matamoros. Los Narcosatanicos, **a drug-dealing black-magic cult, had been kidnapping and sacrificing victims,** whose remains they boiled in a cauldron for a drink they believed kept them safe from the police. That was disproven once they were arrested for turning between sixteen and twenty-six unsuspecting victims into a cartel cannibal brew.

# At least the modern versions are a bit more discerning.

Even during the Middle East's chaotic eleventh century, the Nizari Ismailis stood out. A Shiite Muslim sect seen as heretical by some, they **fended off enemies with *hashashin*: hashish-eating, knife-wielding fanatics**. Marco Polo wrote that any neighboring ruler who "gave umbrage" to them "were put to death." Before being taken out by the Mongols, the Nizari Ismailis so terrified their rivals that even the feared sultan Saladin isolated himself in a tower after nearly being killed by hashashin. Their infamy lives on in modern-day murderers for hire, better known in English as "assassins."

# This brings a whole new meaning to "Thug life."

Say you're a traveler crossing India in the seventeenth or eighteenth century. Your companions seem like jolly good chaps. Then one or more of those chaps quietly throttles you in the night before stealing your possessions. This was all part of an ancient Indian secret society called the Thuggees, who worshipped the goddess of destruction, Kali. **Their faith was less about temples and prayer than it was about serial murder, strangulation, and looting.** The Thugs were largely exterminated by the British in the 1830s. But you should still be a bit suspicious of that intense-looking stranger with the rope who *really* wants to travel with you.

# Saying "no" to the wrong person can cost you your life.

The Chinese cult Church of the Almighty God started in the early 1990s. A woman named Zhao Weishan proclaimed herself the returned Jesus Christ and gathered followers behind her apocalyptic, anti-government message. Despite crackdowns, the cult kept growing, in part through aggressive recruitment. One night in 2014, members tried to convince a woman at a McDonald's in Zhaoyuan to join. When she refused, **they beat her to death with chairs and a mop.** Two of the killers were executed. For some reason, the court did not believe their argument that the completely random, innocent victim was, in fact, a demon in disguise.

> *"We're never gonna get rid of crazy people. They've been around for thousands of years—they'll continue to be around; they'll continue to do horrible things."*
> —MICHAEL MOORE

## Do not try this at home.

In 2016, a twenty-six-year-old man started acting out in ways that disturbed his north London family. He bit people, **claimed there was a snake inside him,** and said he was going to cut off his penis. Rather than take him for psychiatric care, the family—who were deeply devoted followers of a church called Jesus Sanctuary Ministries—spent three days trying to "cure" him by tying him down and praying over him. Oddly enough, this DIY exorcism did nothing to cure the man, who ultimately died of dehydration.

## Did the devil make them do it?

Anneliese Michel, a deeply religious young woman raised in a very Catholic Bavarian family, started suffering from epilepsy and depression as a teenager. She began hearing voices and was unable to be around anything Christian, from crosses to churches, so clearly, she was possessed by Satan. In 1975, two priests stopped Michel's medical treatment and began **a grueling exorcism to purge the multiple demons supposedly living inside her.** After undergoing close to seventy rituals, Michel died on July 1, 1976, from malnutrition and dehydration. Her parents and the priests were convicted of negligent homicide.

# Some killers don't
# need a reason.

In April 2017, Richard Allen called his wife from the jail where he was being held on suspicion of murdering two teenage girls on a hiking trail in Delphi, Indiana. According to prosecutors, he confessed. According to Allen's lawyers, not only did he *not* confess, but the girls had actually been **murdered by members of a white supremacist pagan cult known as Odinists** as part of a ritual sacrifice. The prosecution found that defense "fanciful," accusing the lawyers of playing to social media before securing a conviction against Allen. Before you get too comfortable, though, you should know that Odinists *have* been tied to multiple murders and terror attacks in recent years.

## There's always a compound.

In many ways, the Branch Davidian sect followed the template of twentieth-century millenarianism groups: a charismatic leader who preached apocalypse prepping, isolation, paranoia, and poor decision-making. Still, no one expected that federal agents would lay siege to the sect's fortified compound near Waco, Texas, for fifty-one days in 1993. Similarly shocking was the whole thing ending in **a massive shootout and the deaths of four agents and eighty-two Branch Davidians.** Proving things can always get worse, there is now a chapel near the compound that was largely funded by crackpot conspiracist Alex Jones.

# Faith alone might not save you.

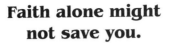

It's good to have faith, but balancing it with a healthy dose of common sense never hurts. James Sakara would not have been the first zealot to get just a wee bit too entranced by his religion's creed. But the twenty-two-year-old pastor of a Zion church in Zambia took it further than most. It was reported that, in 2021, Sakara **talked his congregation into burying him alive.** He promised the faithful he would be resurrected like Jesus Christ after three days. It didn't turn out that way.

## SURVIVAL TIP

In the unlikely (but not impossible!) event that you find yourself buried alive, first do the thing that will feel impossible: don't panic. Conserve your oxygen with deep breaths (no yelling). If you have the room and dexterity, try to protect your face with a piece of clothing, then use your feet to kick through the coffin lid. Use your hands to move the loose dirt around you and away from your face until you break through the surface. And be prepared to scare some people as you rise from your grave.

# Doomsday cults are bad for everyone.

In its early days during the 1980s and 1990s, Aum Shinrikyo was your average Buddhist-Hindu-apocalypse cult. Its tens of thousands of members, concentrated in Japan, were encouraged to sign everything over to their "enlightened" leader Shoko Asahara and even paid for pieces of his hair. Then, on March 20, 1995, **the group left bags filled with sarin nerve gas on crowded Tokyo subway trains**—supposedly to bring about the end of the world—killing twelve and leaving thousands injured. Even after Asahara and several other followers were executed, the cult carried on, though without the leader's holy hair.

# Look out for flaming red flags.

The Movement for the Restoration of the Ten Commandments of God started in Rwanda in the late 1970s as a Roman Catholic cult based around appearances of the Virgin Mary. Eventually, the group split from the church, built up membership in Uganda, and created its own theology based on the end of the world. The date of the supposed apocalypse kept changing, but they finally settled on 2000. When nothing happened, **the cult leaders set fires at multiple sites in Uganda in a mass murder that killed close to 800 people**. More than 500 of those, including children, were burned alive in a church that had its doors and windows nailed shut.

# These are not your usual Mormons.

The Church of Jesus Christ of Latter-Day Saints has many squabbling sects. But the Church of the Lamb of God was the most murdery. Founded in 1971 by Ervil LeBaron—who was excommunicated from his brother's own breakaway polygamist cult—the church set up in Mexico. There, the so-called "Mormon Manson" set about eliminating his enemies, largely imagined. After racking up at least **twenty murders, including two people in a 1974 military-style assault on a rival polygamist compound run by his brother,** LeBaron died in prison in 1981, likely by suicide. But his followers kept on believing and killing for years. According to one: "Everyone is an infidel if they don't believe what you believe."

# Born to be evil?

Though most American biker gangs are made up of harmless motorcyclists blowing off steam, some have proven to be dangerous. Hundreds of outlaw biker gangs are typified by violent conflict, arcane hierarchies, and viciously enforced rules of conduct that rival the most fanatic cults. They battle over turf, real and imagined insults, and even minor disagreements. Underlying the gangs' hellraising and road racing is **an underworld of drug and weapons trafficking.** One shootout between multiple gangs and police in Waco, Texas, in 2015 left nine bikers dead and 177 arrested. So maybe skip that biker bar with the rustic charm on your next road trip.

# This isn't how Buddhism works.

Before convincing people to join his desert cult, Michael Roach gained riches running a diamond business and enlightenment as an ordained Tibetan Buddhist monk. He merged his interests by teaching people how Buddhist ideas led to wealth. In 2000, he founded the Diamond Mountain retreat center in Arizona. Rumors swirled about weird cultic rituals. But the center made headlines in 2012, when **Ian Thorson was found dead from exposure in the desert nearby.** His wife, Christie McNally, was found alive but delirious. Two months prior, the couple had been exiled from Diamond Mountain—where McNally taught and was previously secretly married to Roach, in violation of Buddhist principles—after disagreements over some of McNally's teachings. Seemingly unaffected, Roach continues to run the retreat and publish books like *The Karma of Love.*

# This cult nearly took down a country.

Many Peruvians who met the Shining Path regretted it. A quasi-Maoist cadre founded by former professor Abimael Guzmán in 1969, the group launched a savage terroristic insurgency in 1980. **The fighting left close to 70,000 dead and nearly destroyed the country.** Though theoretically Communist in origin, Shining Path followers were more fanatically dedicated to Guzmán himself, who called himself President Gonzalo, and to his philosophy of "Gonzalo Thought." Their campaign gradually wound down after Guzman's capture in 1992. After all, what is a cult without its guru?

## He just needed a little
## more proof.

To Flat-Earthers, it makes perfect sense that the Earth is laid out flat and surrounded by a massive ice wall. The ferocity of that belief and resistance to outside ideas have given its people the zeal of isolated cultists. And some of them have met untimely ends because of it. Take Michael "Mad Mike" Hughes, for example. On February 22, 2020, **Hughes died in the crash of a homemade rocket** he launched in the hope of going high enough to take pictures that showed no curvature, thus proving the Earth's flatness. That dream came to an end when his rocket's parachutes failed to deploy.

## Respect for human life isn't high
## on the Nazis' priority list.

In 1961, Paul Schaefer—a Nazi-sympathizing ex-Wehrmacht soldier suspected of child molestation—founded a remote colony in Chile where he could run his own creepy quasi-Christian cult. There, he allegedly hosted Nazi war criminal Josef Mengele and **burned down a nearby convent to grab the nuns' land**. Based on Schaefer's grotesque bona fides, it already looked like his "Colonia Dignidad" was going to be one of the worst places on Earth. Then Schaefer agreed to give dictator Augusto Pinochet a place where political prisoners could be detained and tortured. When finally arrested at an Argentinian hideout in 2005, Schaefer kept asking, "Why?"

# A lawless place doesn't always make a good hideout.

In 2015, a community of self-identified "anarcho-capitalists" started gathering in Acapulco for annual conferences called "Anarchapulco." These were feverish rallies for the cult-ish circle around cryptocurrency investor Jeff Berwick, whose conference attracted **a mix of anti-state libertarians, fellow crypto enthusiasts, and expatriates on the run.** One of the latter was John Galton (not his real name), an anarchist fleeing U.S. drug charges who, in 2019, was gunned down in Acapulco. (By then, the city was starting to transition from devil-may-care vacation mecca to semi-stateless crime mecca.) No one is sure why Galton was killed, but it certainly put a damper on the anarchy.

# Can you really be too careful?

In a shocking and inexplicable tragedy in a small village in northeast Thailand in early 2018, five seemingly healthy young men died in their sleep. Stories spread about similar deaths in nearby villages. Suspicions fell on the ghost of a widowed woman, who the deeply superstitious villagers thought was **seducing sleeping men to become her lovers in the afterlife.** To keep the alluring spirit off their scent, men started wearing women's clothes and makeup. For good measure, households put up scarecrows with giant penises and signs proclaiming, "There is no man here." It may seem like a bit much, but they would argue it worked—the strange deaths stopped.

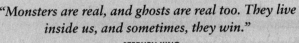

## Never trust a fox.

Japanese legend says that many centuries ago, an emperor was bewitched by a beautiful young woman. His royal astrologer warned him she was really an evil nine-tailed fox masquerading as human. Discovered, the fox ran but was **shot full of arrows by the emperor's men.** This, according to the lore, turned her into a rock. Known as the "killing stone" for the fox's murderous tendencies, the six-foot-high rock at Nikko National Park broke apart in 2022, supposedly freeing the fox and portending doom for humanity.

## No, it's totally true— I read it online.

The urban legend of Slenderman first appeared in 2009 in an online forum called Something Awful. That doesn't mean that this tall, faceless phantasm—known for creeping out terminally online kids before disappearing—never crosses into the real world. In 2014, **a teenaged girl was stabbed nearly to death** in the Wisconsin woods by a pair of twelve-year-old classmates. The girls apparently wanted to impress Slenderman. This would have been challenging, since the Slenderman character is always rendered as mouthless and faceless, and thus has no obvious means of expressing approval or disapproval.

# Are you playing or being played?

If you were an avid gamer who lived in Portland, Oregon, circa 1981, you may have heard of an arcade game named Polybius. Rumors spread that it was really a secret government experiment and that black-suited agents were supposedly seen opening the machines to study the data. The same rumors said that they checked on players, who began having **seizures, nightmares, and nausea,** and even attempted suicide. Evidently, Polybius disappeared after about a month. But who knows what games out there today are actually military-industrial complex mind control tests in disguise?

# You can visit your own grave.

Every now and then, the Internet provides something useful besides recipes and new ways to feel bad about your lack of accomplishments. Thanks to the good people operating the website Find a Grave, you can now look for the final resting places of everyone from famous people (Jim Morrison, Karl Marx, and Princess Diana are all worth a gander) to your Aunt Edna (somebody should really leave flowers). You can also look for **the gravesite of somebody who has your name.** Creepy? Absolutely. But as memento mori selfies go, it cannot be beat. Unless, of course, you fear a self-fulfilling prophecy à la Marcus Garvey (see page 159).

# This "Gloomy Sunday" might be your last.

After Hungarian composer Rezső Seress was dumped by his girlfriend, he did the expected thing: he wrote a sad melody about how he felt. But the lyrics Seress's poet friend László Jávor (also recently single) penned for 1933's surprisingly popular "Gloomy Sunday" made it less a breakup ballad than a suicide ode. It went: "Angels have no thought / of ever returning you, / Would they be angry / If I thought of joining you?" **Dozens of suicides have been attributed to the song,** including that of Seress' ex, who was supposedly found holding the song's sheet music after taking poison. In 1968, Seress joined her by jumping from a high window. Listeners should exercise caution.

# Why would the fiction writer make that up?

In the nineteenth century, it was a common belief that, every so often, people just burst into flames. Bad luck, but what are you going to do? Charles Dickens even used "spontaneous human combustion" as a shocking way to dispose of a character in the novel *Bleak House*. According to science-y thought at the time, **people were more likely to expire this way if they had been drinking heavily,** because a body filled with alcohol is more fire-prone. Odds are good there were other factors in suspected cases, but anyone planning to go on a bender should keep matches and lighters far, far away just in case.

# The kiss of death.

Have you heard the urban legend about a person with a peanut allergy dying from a kiss? It happened in 2012. Myriam Ducré-Lemay began **having trouble breathing after kissing her boyfriend,** who had recently eaten a peanut butter sandwich. She had not yet told him about her allergy and did not have her Medic Alert bracelet or medication on her. Ducré-Lemay went into cerebral anoxia and died not long after. It might not be romantic, but discussing food allergies before locking lips might save a life.

# Want to meet up at the Devil's Tree?

Folklore in southern Florida's Port St. Lucie says the gnarled old oak tree in Oak Hammock Park was the site of a brutal murder, after which satanists congregated there to hold ritual sacrifices. In truth, the so-called "Devil's Tree" *was* near the site of some evil doings. In 1972, former sheriff's deputy-turned-serial-killer Gerard Schaefer murdered two teenage girls, Susan Place and Georgia Jessup, mutilating and decapitating their bodies before burying them in the park. **Schaefer used his badge to lure as many as twenty-six victims to remote places,** which is a good thing to keep in mind should you find yourself following police orders into unpopulated areas.

## Beware a man who carries around a hatchet.

Urban legends and Internet fame came together in 2013 when Kai Lawrence (real name: Caleb Lawrence McGillvary) became a media sensation. In a reverse of spooky stories about killer hitchhikers in the backseat, Lawrence—an unhoused surfer— told a California news station a dubious story about **using his trusty hatchet to save pedestrians from a psychotic man** who gave him a ride. Six years after his fifteen minutes of fame were up, Lawrence was convicted of murder for beating a seventy-three-year-old New Jersey man to death. He claimed self-defense for that attack, too, but this time, inconsistencies in his story landed him in jail.

## Let's not give murderers any more ideas.

One of Japan's more famous urban legends was about the Alice Killer. Starting around 1999, tales circulated about a series of murders with no connection except for **a playing card left by each body with the name "Alice" written on it in the victim's blood.** It was a story that sounded like something out of a movie. But fantasy became reality in 2003, when Alfredo Galán Sotillo was convicted of murdering six people in Madrid, Spain. He sometimes left playing cards on the bodies, becoming known as the Playing Card Killer, though he didn't take the extra step of writing "Alicia" on any of them.

# Don't mess with
# the dead.

As suggested by the name of Iowa's Villisca Axe Murder House, it was the location of a gruesome multiple murder: In 1912, six children and two adults were killed by having their skulls crushed while lying in bed. The killer was never caught. Years later, the house opened as a morbid tourist attraction for people who like the idea of being around spirits of the dead. In 2014, some friends looking for "recreational paranormal" fun **discovered one of their party dead from a stabbing** that supposedly happened at the same time as the 1912 murders. The death was attributed to suicide, but paranormal investigators believe otherwise.

# Even happiness has
# its limits.

Disneyland might be the Happiest Place on Earth, but there is a haunted mansion's worth of spooky urban legends that swirl around the tourist attraction. There are also a few unfortunate real-life deaths, including that of Bogden Delaurot. In 1973, the teenager and his little brother, Dorian, wanted to stay at Disneyland longer, so they hid out on Tom Sawyer's Island until the park closed. Once the coast was clear, Bogden swam across the moat with his brother on his back. Before making it over, **Bogden went underwater and never reappeared.** Even though the younger Delaurot was the one who couldn't swim, he survived.

# Two words: sewer alligators.

Too many people assume urban legends are not real. Stories about alligators escaping into New York City's sewers and growing to huge sizes have floated around for years, cropping up in tabloid papers and horror movies. And they're based in truth: **In 1935, an 8-foot-long alligator showed up in an East Harlem storm drain.** As recently as 2023, a live alligator (that suspiciously ingested a bathtub stopper) was captured in Brooklyn's Prospect Park. That's pretty far from Florida, where you expect that kind of thing to happen. Going forward, keep your eyes on that sewer grate.

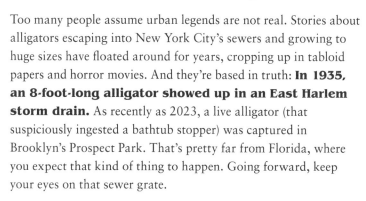

## SURVIVAL TIP

The best way to survive an alligator attack is to always and forever avoid alligators. Thankfully, unprovoked attacks are rare. So just stay away from the babies, and don't go skinny dipping in their territory at night. (How do you know it's their territory? If you have to ask, it's too risky.) When facing an alligator on dry land, run away fast in a straight line (not a zig-zag) to tire it out.

# Sometimes, we are our own
# worst enemies.

Homer and Langley Collyer were brothers who lived most of their lives after their father's 1919 abandonment in a Harlem mansion. Paranoia, eccentricity, scavenging, and hoarding took over their lonely existence for decades. Responding in 1947 to reports of a dead body, police discovered a rotting home jammed with junk and two corpses. **Langley had died after springing one of his own booby traps,** after which Homer (paralyzed and blind) starved to death surrounded by hundreds of thousands of newspapers he could not read.

# It was the TV death
# nobody ever saw.

According to some, a 1971 episode of *The Dick Cavett Show* gave viewers a rare sight: a guest dying on stage. That's not exactly how things went down. Cavett was taping an interview with alternative-health pioneer and publisher J. I. Rodale, who wanted the host to eat asparagus boiled in urine. **Rodale then made an odd noise and stopped breathing.** He was never revived. Since the show was not broadcast live, the producers decided not to air it. Rodale's last pronouncement on the show was that he would "live to be a hundred."

# There are no age limits
# on murder.

John F. Kennedy assassination-theory devotees often point to the people connected to the conspiracy who ended up dead. John Rosselli, a mobster born in Italy in 1905 who worked with Al Capone before running the casino skim in Las Vegas, was one of them. He also testified to the Senate in 1976 about his involvement in CIA plans to kill Fidel Castro. When a friend asked Rosselli if he feared for his life, the chatty Mafioso replied, "Who'd want to kill an old man like me?" Not long afterward, **his body was found stuffed into a 55-gallon drum** submerged off the coast of northern Miami.

# This is one hail of
# a way to go.

In 1942, a forest ranger happened upon a frozen lake filled with over 200 skeletons in a remote Himalayan valley in northeast India. The cause of death was a mystery, though a local folk story claimed the skeletons of Roopkund Lake belonged to pilgrims headed to the shrine of a mountain goddess who killed them in a fit of rage around 850 CE. Research in 2004 discovered a more likely culprit: hail. Forensic analysis showed **the victims all died from skull fractures caused by round objects.** This led to the conclusion that a downpour of nine-inch-wide hailstones had caused the massacre, though that doesn't entirely negate the angry-goddess theory.

# Why take a chance
# on a curse?

One of the most stunning sights on Venice, Italy's, Grand Canal is Palazzo Dario. Built in 1479 in the Venetian Gothic style, it was painted several times by Monet. But the gorgeous palazzo built over a Templar cemetery also seems cursed, leaving inhabitants ruined or dead. The daughter, son-in-law, and grandson of the namesake noble who built Dario came to ugly ends (murder, suicide, and assassination, respectively). **Other owners faced scandals, family tragedies, addiction, more suicides, and more murders.** The Latin inscription on its façade translates to "Giovanni Dario to the Genius of the City," but some have created a fittingly macabre anagram from it that translates to "I bring treacherous ruins to those who live under this roof."

# The reality is creepier.

There is one urban legend everyone knows: A teenaged couple is making out in their car on a lovers' lane when the music is interrupted by an announcement that a convict with a hook hand has escaped. "Oh no," the girl says. "Don't worry, baby," the boy says. Later, the boy discovers a hook hanging on the door handle. The story started circulating in the 1950s, spurred by fears over the very real "Moonlight Murders." During three months in 1946, the small "twin city" of Texarkana—with one town in Texas and a neighboring town across the state line in Arkansas—**saw five people shot dead, four in unprovoked attacks on couples in cars.** The "Phantom Killer" was never caught but lived on in the indelible campfire story.

# Yellowstone is terrifying
# for so many reasons.

Many urban legends about the law are just wrong, like the belief that you cannot be charged if a victim declines to press charges (that's up to the prosecutor). One that might be true, though, is the so-called "Zone of Death." Nobody lives in this 50-square-mile section of Yellowstone National Park. That means, if you get murdered there, **your killer could invoke their constitutional right to a jury by their peers and be released because there are no peers.** Legal scholars debate if this loophole is valid, but why take a chance?

## The faeries did it?

Belief in faeries is widespread in Ireland, a country steeped in legend. Twenty-six-year-old Bridget Cleary was fascinated with them, which may explain her ordeal. Returning to the Tipperary cottage she shared with her husband, Michael, one day in 1895, she fell ill. The doctor diagnosed bronchitis, but **Michael was convinced his wife had been replaced by a changeling** (a creature faeries use to replace a stolen human). His proof? She seemed a couple inches taller than the woman he'd married. Bridget survived a quasi-exorcism involving a local "fairy doctor," only for Michael to burn her alive a few days later. He went to jail for manslaughter, not murder, because he killed his wife out of genuine belief.

# Index
of Horrors

Exposure, 48, 127, 130, 135, 154, 178, 181, 234
Extermination, 179

## F

Falling, 11
Falling trees, 138, 139, 141
Feces-related incident, 70
Fire (accidental), 7, 19, 27, 82, 139, 169
Fire (intentional), 89, 151, 204, 232, 235
Flooding, 134
Flooding (beer), 146
Friendly fire, 81, 172

## G

Going overboard, 57
Goose attack, 70
Goring, 65, 96
Gun death (accidental), 15, 30, 39, 40, 109, 149, 212, 215, 217
Gun death (intentional), 162, 195, 206, 210

## H

Hail, 245
Harness malfunction, 74
Hazardous living conditions, 19
Hazardous working conditions, 62, 63, 73, 81
Heatstroke, 127, 142
Hiking, 135
Hit and run, 191
Hit job, 199, 201, 145
Hoarding, 244
Holiday heart syndrome, 35
Human bites, 106
Human sacrifice, 146, 148, 166, 226
Hypothermia, 214
Hysteria, 36, 155

## I

Impalement, 39, 88, 116
Infection, 171, 183
Insomnia, 36
Intoxication, 4, 75

## K

Kamikaze, 181
Kidnapping, 217, 219, 230

## L

Landmines, 24
Laughter, 150, 184
Lightning strike, 123

## M

Malfunction, 10
Malpractice, 13, 34, 190, 191
Matricide, 208
Mauling, 92, 95, 99, 100, 102, 107, 109, 116, 117
Memento mori, 238
Meteorite, 123
Mind control, 238
Misdiagnosis, 12, 33
Mistaken identity, 188
Model-plane accident, 29
Monkey aggression, 101, 111
Mosquito-borne illness, 103, 114
Motorcycle accident, 50
Mutilation, 111, 194, 196, 218
Mythological creature, 237

## N

Nerve agent, 198, 232

## O

Obesity, 37
Obsessive gaming, 28
Organized crime, 208
Overdose, 18
Overindulgence, 108, 153

## P

Pandemic, 57, 177
Parachute failure, 79
Paranormal death, 236, 242
Parasite, 100, 113
Pedestrian death, 44
Piercing, 31
Plague, 129, 153
Plunging, 15, 17, 21, 92, 125
Pneumonia, 161